# Beyond

## THE MUSIC LESSON

# Beyond

## THE MUSIC LESSON

### HABITS OF
### SUCCESSFUL
### SUZUKI
### FAMILIES

CHRISTINE E. GOODNER

© 2017 Christine E. Goodner

*Beyond the Music Lesson: The Habits of Successful Suzuki Families*
First Edition, May 2017
Brookside Suzuki Strings, LLC
Hillsboro, Oregon

Editing: Shayla Eaton, CuriouserEditing.com
Publishing & Design Services: Melinda Martin, MartinPublishingServices.com

ISBN: 978-0-9991192-0-4 (print), 978-0-9991192-1-1 (epub)

*To my parents*
*who have given me a childhood filled with music,*
*family, laughter, and love.*


*I wouldn't be who I am today without you.*


*To Hannah and Samantha*
*who taught me what it means to be a parent*
*and have grown into amazing young women.*


*I am proud to call you my daughters.*

# Contents

# Disclaimer

This work represents the view of its author, and does not necessarily represent the view of the International Suzuki Association or its regional associations. These materials are not intended to replace authorized Suzuki® Method teacher training or study with a qualified Suzuki teacher.

# Preface

*Beyond the Music Lesson* is a discussion about how to develop the habits and mindset to succeed once you have committed to Suzuki lessons.

If you are still trying to decide if this method is for you and are looking for detailed information about what the Suzuki method is, there are a few good resources for you to read. I recommend starting with *Nurtured by Love* by Shinichi Suzuki and visiting www.SuzukiAssociation.org to learn more about the method and how it started.

This book was written to address the more hands-on, day-to-day parts of the Suzuki method. What does it take beyond attending lessons to be successful? What does it look like to make the method work in our everyday lives? What is the mindset, or approach, that successful families take to make it work for them?

I get many calls for prospective violin and viola students from parents requesting more information. Some parents tell me, "My child seems interested in music (or the violin), and we want to *try it out* to see if they will like it."

There are many activities that are appropriate for our children to try out and to give us a good idea of what their interests are. As a parent, I completely understand this approach. We often sign up our kids for many different types of activities to expose them to a wide variety of things and to see what they enjoy.

A word of caution, though.

*Taking Suzuki lessons is not like that.* The whole premise of the method, and the secret to its success, is that your child will be learning an instrument the way a young child learns a language. They need to be immersed in hearing it, seeing others do it, and practicing it daily—then they will gradually learn to "speak" the language themselves.

Imagine you want your child to be bilingual. What kind of commitment would that take? It would certainly be different than exposing them to gymnastics class. The Suzuki method is about immersing our children in music, not exposing them to it.

To do this, you don't have to commit to your child playing their instrument until they are thirty. We never know what our children will be doing twenty years from now. However, if we just "try out" music lessons, it lowers the chances that they will still be playing their instrument that far in the future.

Research shows that when students start lessons with a long-term commitment, their ability to play the instrument years later is dramatically higher than those who begin with a short-term commitment in mind.

How can that be? I would argue that a short-term commitment is not enough to motivate us to adopt the habits and mindset that lead to success, which are discussed in this book.

As you will see, there are many aspects of making this method work. It takes an all-in learning approach, rather than dipping our toes in the water to try it out.

Before we talk about all the other pieces of this process, this is the big concept to wrap our brains around as parents: Do we want our children to learn to play an instrument to the best of their ability? Do we want them to make and appreciate beautiful music? Do we want our children to develop character qualities that will help them succeed later in life, whatever they choose to do?

If the answer is yes, then this process is worth committing to. Whatever path your child takes with music and in their lives, what they learn through their time as a Suzuki student (and what we learn as parents supporting them) will serve them well.

Make a commitment to view this as a long-term process, and you have already taken one step toward helping your child be successful!

# Introduction

The Suzuki method is a way of teaching and learning music developed by Shinichi Suzuki in post-World War II Japan. He observed and studied how young children learned their native language and applied what he observed to help children better learn music, initially on the violin. Suzuki emphasized concepts like: creating an environment for children where they are surrounded by beautiful music; treating and teaching each child as if they can learn to play (rather than testing them for aptitude, which was standard practice at the time); and playing music that has already been learned to the point that it becomes automatic and can be played with ease (much as children learn a word and keep using it over and over until it is part of their vocabulary).

The Suzuki method, in my experience, is technique-based. It teaches that character development is at least as important as the development of musical skills. It can be a common misperception that Suzuki teachers do not teach students to read music, but that is not true of any well-trained, modern Suzuki teacher I know. Many of our nation's orchestra musicians, as well as many soloists, started their training in the Suzuki method. I like to think of it as a method that develops the whole child—not just a few skills that a child knows.

I was a Suzuki student, starting lessons at the age of two and a half. There are parts of being successful at the Suzuki method that I take for granted, because I've never known anything else. As a teacher, though, I am often reminded that there are many parts of what make this method work that are new ideas to the families I work with. Some of them require changing how a family plans their day, or how they interact when working with each other one-on-one. As a teacher, it's my job to explain how families can help their child be successful at studying their instrument through small, day-to-day changes and through shifting their mindset about their role in the process.

As a Suzuki parent, I struggled with all of this myself. So I want to do everything I can to make it easier for the families I work with. That has caused me to spend the last eighteen years learning all that I can about what it is that makes families successful, rather than struggle. The more I have learned about the topic, the more I am able to help the families in my studio. I'm excited to share some of what I have learned with you in this book.

The longer I teach the Suzuki method, the more emphasis I put on parent education, or helping parents understand the process of helping their child succeed. Learning an instrument is difficult. Without the right information and expectations, many people struggle or even give up. That is not the outcome I want as a teacher. When I tell people what my profession is, the most common response I get is: "Oh, I played an instrument as a kid . . . I really wish my parents hadn't let me quit." How sad! And yet, some families really struggle so it is easy to see why this happens.

Ideally, a family starting out with lessons will find many resources on how to make lessons and practicing work best for their family. Books like this one have a lot of good information on how to be successful before lessons are ever started. It's so much easier to start off on the right foot than to develop bad habits and give up.

If you have already begun lessons, please don't wait until you are at a crisis point to keep learning more about how to help your child succeed. Continue to learn about how to help your child be successful all along the way. —

Whichever place you are in—whether you are just starting out or simply finding new ideas—I hope you find this resource helpful and encouraging.

## Real Life Struggles

There are a lot of issues I hear from families who are struggling: How do we keep students engaged in learning music? How do we make the day-to-day reality of practicing less of a chore? How do we keep students motivated? How do we keep parents engaged? How do we keep families involved and help them understand that all the time, effort, and sacrifice are worth it? How do we make practice and doing hard things easier for children and as painless as possible for parents?

Learning a musical instrument, especially through the Suzuki method, has many rewards. Beyond becoming proficient at a musical instrument, music teaches students discipline, hard work, and perseverance and develops who they are as people. Your job as a Suzuki parent is an important part of this process. It is definitely worth the effort!

## How I Got Started on This Topic

Over the last few years, I have been rethinking how I equip parents to help their student succeed. How do I better explain everything involved in making this work in their daily lives? I had a real wake-up call a number of years ago when I found that some families I worked with were surprised at my expectations for them a few years into our time together. I felt that I had explained the importance of practice, listening, group classes, and all the other parts of what makes this method work but realized I was making a lot of assumptions about what parents already knew and believed. I was sprinkling in information on how to be successful here and there, but I wasn't addressing it directly enough to help the parents I worked with grasp the importance of what I was saying.

This experience made me look at the process I had for introducing new families to my expectations and even more importantly, what makes this process work for everyone. I wanted to find information to share beyond my own instructions—information that shares the best practices of those who have made it work for their own children or students. It's powerful to hear from other families, teachers, and experts about what helped them (or the families they worked with) succeed.

I set off to discover what mindset I could help families develop in order to minimize struggles and stick with the process. What do other teachers, experts, and families say helped them the most? What patterns could I find that set people off on the right path? How do I help people develop the tools they need when it becomes clear that this is hard work and a long process? And most of all, how do I help them understand the big picture so they understand why learning an instrument is worth all this effort?

## My Story

First, let me share part of my story.

My interest in helping Suzuki parents succeed comes in part because I consider myself something of a Suzuki parent failure. I had my kids while in college so I was a younger mom. In fact, I was just starting out as a Suzuki teacher myself, when my oldest was four years old and we started violin together. I was her practice parent and her teacher. Some people make this work beautifully, but it did not work well for us.

I'm not sure there is a way to accurately describe the struggle between a very opinionated and headstrong four-year-old and a very inexperienced and idealistic mom/teacher. We struggled! There were some epic showdowns where you could practically *see* the standoff happening like in an old Western movie, with the tumbleweed rolling by, as we sat in suspense wondering who would win the battle this time. I so wanted to do it "just right" and she so wanted to avoid how hard it felt and most likely the pressure she felt from me.

It's a funny story now, because that daughter is twenty years old and puts her (self-admitted) headstrong ways into working toward productive goals, like graduating college a year early, which she is scheduled to do this year. As a parent, I have learned how to pick battles and how to focus on the long-term outcomes I want versus focusing on the little things being done just so. Our days of practice showdowns are far behind us, and her musical story turned out well in the end too.

This daughter spent her school years as a musician. After a not-too-successful attempt at Suzuki violin with me, she studied cello for a while with a member of the Oregon Symphony, and then the flute, which she played in the band through most of high school.

Midway through high school, she found her real musical love: singing. Specifically, musical theater. She spent her high school days singing and dancing on the high school stage. Her sister followed a very similar path, minus the flute, and continues to do musical theater in high school now.

Both of my daughters love music. They kept doing it through high school and will always value music as a part of their lives.

Really, our story is one of success. I raised two musicians: ones who understand hard work, discipline, cooperation with others, and a love of music. But, still I often wish I could go back to those early days of practicing together knowing what I know now. I think we would have had an easier time of it. We would understand each other more. I know that I would feel so much more confident about what I was doing. I often wonder if my daughters would have stayed with the violin if I could have been a better Suzuki parent.

And, while I wish it were different for us, through our struggles I have developed a passion to help other parents avoid our mistakes and be more successful. I have made it my passion to help Suzuki families focus on working well together without giving up.

If you are struggling through practice with your child, you are not alone. If I could go back and say something to that idealistic and frustrated parent that I was, I would say: "Talk to other parents so you know you're not alone. Read everything you can on the subject, look online for practice games and ideas (if Pinterest existed back then, it would have been an amazing resource). Remember to focus on the kind of human being you are raising rather than getting bogged down in doing everything perfectly. It will be okay."

The longer I teach and research this topic, the better equipped I feel to help parents I work with do the same. I know if I went back now and started over with my own kids, we could make it work much more easily. I think that's partly because I would be better able to handle all the to-dos and all the strong emotions, but mostly because what I've learned along the way has a lot more to do with focusing on *whom to be* instead of *what to do.*

I've learned that being someone who prioritizes music, who values mastery, who listens to great music, and who is a part of their music community is a much more helpful approach than trying to do a big list of tasks. Yes, there are still things to do—we're just kidding ourselves if we pretend there isn't. It's just that who we are becoming comes first and if some to-dos don't get done, we keep going because who we are working to become is the real goal.

This doesn't only apply to music lessons and the Suzuki method. Who I choose to be as a parent, who we choose to be as a family, and who I try to develop my children to be (keeping in mind who they are in the first place) is what makes for success.

I realize that when working with my own children, I should have focused on whom we were trying to be and not get bogged down in all the tasks that felt daunting and overwhelming. I hope through the interviews, research, and personal stories in this book, you feel the same thing is true for you.

## Why This Message Needs to Be Heard

I end up having a lot of conversations, both online and in person with other teachers. We often talk about what books we ask parents to read to learn more about the method. Of course, many teachers ask families to read *Nurtured by Love* by Dr. Suzuki, but what next? What resource gives a good picture of how the Suzuki method looks today, here and now, and in our own lives?

To that question, there are many varying opinions but no consensus that I've ever heard. Certain books are good for technique, and others give some good insights into part of the process. But what resource addresses the question, "How does the Suzuki method look in modern times, in our lives today?" That's what I've been looking for.

Since I haven't found a resource that does this well for me, over the past few years, I have written my own set of parent education materials for the families in my studio. I try to answer questions before they come up about practice, the environment we create for our children to *practice in*, why playing in a group or with other people is important, why repetition and review is going to be a big part of our work together, and other such subjects.

Giving out more detailed materials like these, I have seen a dramatic change in how new families approach lessons and how successful they are at navigating the process from beginner and beyond. This book combines those materials with interviews and success stories to help answer the question, "How do we make the Suzuki method work for our family today?"

I hope teachers will find this book a useful resource for sharing with the families in their studios and most of all, I hope parents will find it encouraging and helpful to set up successful Suzuki habits in their homes.

*Special Invitation: If you find this book useful and would like to join a community of Suzuki parents and teachers who discuss these topics in-depth, join us in the Suzuki Triangle community on Facebook. We'd love to have you join in the conversation and feel supported.*

# The Mindset for Suzuki Success

The Suzuki method is so incredible that I could fill this whole book with stories about students, teachers, and families who can attest to the fact that their lives have been changed for the better because of how this method has impacted them in musical and nonmusical ways alike.

Professional orchestra players and a number of well-known soloists (Rachel Barton Pine, Ray Chen, and Brian Lewis to name a few) got their start through the Suzuki method, so there's proof that it works for raising professional musicians and great adults who pursue other careers alike.

Suzuki parents: all the effort and hard work you put into this is worth it. There are a lot of tasks you will be given each week in order to parent a Suzuki student—practice every day, attend lessons and group classes, listen to recordings daily, and attend recitals and performances. Your teacher will ask you things like, "Did you listen this week?" or "How many days did you practice?" or "Are you able to come to XYZ event/class/workshop?" Our lives are already busy, and this can seem like a huge list of things to do.

But I would like to say to all the parents reading this that it's not really about all that—it's not about what your child does today that is most important. Ten years from now, the fact that your child practiced on a random Monday in July is not a life-changing event. But who your child has become because they practiced daily *is*. This process is about more than a list of things to do—it's about who we are raising children to be.

Ten years from now, the fact that your child has both the self-discipline to get what they need done but the grace for themselves to know not every day is going to be exactly ideal—now that is life-changing!

Ten years from now, when your child encounters a big obstacle or goal in life and knows they can succeed if they just break it down in little pieces and work on things one at a time—that is a skill that sets them apart.

When asked what they learned from studying the Suzuki method, adult Suzuki students don't usually answer with the names of pieces or by listing instrumental techniques; instead, they list character traits: discipline, love for music, ability to break big problems into small pieces, persistence . . .

This is the life-changing work we're really doing when we practice bow holds, attend institutes, and practice those review pieces yet again. As parents and teachers, let's focus more on what's important:

**Practicing daily:** Yes, because of whom we become when we do it (not because everything was done perfectly every day).

**Listening to our music:** Yes, because we learn that when we need to learn something, we can immerse ourselves in the knowledge of those who have already learned it and get a clear picture of where we will go. Not to mention, we will gain an appreciation for beautiful music.

**Attending events in the Suzuki community (like group classes/workshops/institutes/camps):** Yes, but not because it's required by the teacher or because it's the thing to do, but because we learn about community, cooperation, and time spent around inspiring people we can learn from in every part of our lives.

Don't worry about doing it all perfectly. Don't worry that your child is going their own speed. Don't worry that today's practice was short and you only got through part of what you should practice. It's not what you practice today that's important—it's what you do over time with the bigger picture in mind.

Pat yourself on the back and be proud that you got the instrument out, that you haven't given up, that you're showing up and making this a part of your life. You are raising a future adult who will benefit from all this in ways you may not see for many years. It is so worth it!

Suzuki is not something we just *do*. We have to have a major shift in mindset in order for it work well. Suzuki is so different from other activities—soccer, swimming, chess club. All of these activities can be done by just showing up and working to improve your skills.

Learning music through the Suzuki method (especially being on the parent side of the equation) takes a different mindset. We have to be open to changing as a parent. Sometimes that means letting go of how we were parented or our default way of reacting under stress. Parents and children work so closely together in this method, so healthy ways of working through conflict are a must. If you feel unsure if you can do this, don't worry—you will learn how along the way.

Just this week, the mother of a three-year-old student I am teaching came to lessons and said, "Suzuki lessons are making me a better parent!" It all works together.

Seek to understand where your child is coming from (even if you think it makes no logical sense) and start working with them from there. I believe that we have to treat our students and our children with respect if we want to have a good working relationship with them. When they feel that from us, they are often more willing to work with us rather than to fight with us.

## Think Long-Term

Another mindset shift is to move toward long-term thinking. Learning an instrument is not an activity that you can try for a month, decide if it's fun and enjoyable, and then let that be your guide as to whether to continue.

Remember that we are learning music much in the same way children learn a language—it's fun and exciting to be successful at it, but it takes a lot of trial and error and a lot of practice. Every moment won't feel fun, but if we step back and see how far we've come and if we start playing songs and play together with others, then it really can be fun. We just need to take a long-term view of our progress.

Daniel Coyle describes a striking example of this in the book *The Talent Code*.[1] The book describes in detail a 1997 study by Gary McPherson, who followed a large group of students from when they started lessons around age seven or eight through high school. He wanted to study why some students succeeded at their instrument and why others didn't. He found some surprising results. There was no clear difference between the students when he studied their day-to-day habits, but when he looked at the questions he had asked students at the start of lessons, he found it there. Students who had made a long-term commitment to studying the instrument (versus a short- or medium-length commitment) had a huge advantage.

In Coyle's book, he quotes McPherson as saying the following about the results: "I couldn't believe my eyes. Progress was determined not by any measurable aptitude or trait, but by a tiny powerful idea the child had before even starting lessons. The differences were staggering. With the same amount of practice, the long-term-commitment group outperformed the short-term-commitment group by 400 percent."[2]

As a Suzuki parent—especially of a very young child—you are setting the expectation with your child for how long they will play their instrument. If you have a long-term commitment to the process, it has a huge impact on your child's commitment level and on their future success.

Parents who just want to "try lessons out" to see if their child thinks it's fun or who ask their child if they want to quit any time the going gets tough are impressing upon their student that this is a short-term commitment on the family's part.

Music lessons are a big (and worthwhile) undertaking. I would encourage you to go into the process with a commitment to stay with it long-term for the greatest chance at success. Of course, your child may switch instruments some day or may develop other interests that make it hard to continue at some point. That's the reality for some students no matter what we do, but setting up the expectation that we are studying music long-term gives your child an advantage. Adopting this mindset from the start—or switching gears now and changing the language you use about the commitment your family has now—is a great idea.

## Developing Mastery

Another important part of the mindset needed for a successful Suzuki experience is to focus on developing mastery. There is something very exciting about learning new music—and sometimes we can confuse learning a new piece of music with making progress on the instrument.

However, in music and especially the Suzuki method, mastery and playing with artistry are a more important judge of success than what piece you can play. It's not how many pieces you know, but how well do you know them that matters most.

Can you play your pieces with a great bow hold? With a beautiful sound (tone)? Do you have the pieces you've learned solidly in your memory so that you can come back to them and master them further (review)?

It's important to know from the start that mastery is one of our goals. Otherwise, progress can feel slow and we might feel impatient to move on to something new too soon.

Don't be in a rush—good teachers will take their time and make sure students are playing solidly. Sometimes, as a parent, it is unclear what needs to happen to master a song. As a teacher, I am always open to the question, "What do we need to improve in order to move on to the next piece?"

Teachers look for a certain level of mastery on each piece of music, keeping the big picture in mind. As teachers, we know that if we move ahead too early, the student is going to struggle with what is coming up in our next set of pieces.

## Keeping Our Bigger Goals in Mind

Successful Suzuki families ask themselves important questions that help keep the end goal in mind. Questions like: What characteristics do we want to train our children to have as they grow up? How will we work with who they are to help develop them into the best version of themselves?

To me, this big-picture thinking is so much more important than whether my students or children become professional musicians or even how advanced of a player they become. We all want our students and children to strive for excellence. I'm not suggesting *not* to aim for that. But it's who we become in the process that really counts.

When we emphasize daily practice, our children learn that being diligent and persistent causes their ability to grow.

When we emphasize listening to the Suzuki recordings, our children learn how to seek out those who have already mastered what they are striving to learn—something that will serve them well no matter what skills they want to learn later in life.

When we emphasize doing our best and setting goals, our children learn how this helps them follow through and achieve success to the best of their ability. This will serve them well in any future goal they have—personal or professional.

This is why it's a good idea to adopt the mindset of successful Suzuki families from the start. This is why it's worth it to keep going even when things aren't easy.

This is why it serves us well to step back and look at why we are learning music. What do we want to see developed in our children when they are in high school and beyond? How will their experience learning their instrument help them do that? Our mindset as Suzuki teachers and parents will help make this happen.

The Suzuki method is about more than a list of things to do to learn an instrument; it's also about who we are raising children to be.

# What Does Success Look Like?

"Successful families work together happily; they find joy in the process. They love the experience and progress at a comfortable pace. They figure out how to be good cheerleaders for their children."

—Sharon Jones

Now that we've covered the kind of mindset that helps Suzuki families succeed, how do we define what success is in this method?

Does it mean that a student graduates from all of the Suzuki books? Does it mean they become a professional musician? Does it mean they get a scholarship to college with their instrument? Or play in the top youth orchestra as a teenager? I would consider all those things to qualify as success, but I also think it's more than that.

Many Suzuki teachers and parents who have raised Suzuki kids would agree that success is more than musical accomplishments, even though those are important too.

Success in this method also includes sticking with something that doesn't come easy. It includes learning how to deal with feelings of not being good at something on the first try and working through frustration. It includes striving to reach your potential and learning confidence through practice. It is learning to play the instrument with ease and also learning to be a person who is sensitive to the world around them.

In order to find out more about how Suzuki teachers define success, I conducted interviews with several experienced and knowledgeable teachers who were able to share their thoughts with me.

First, Suzuki Early Childhood Education (SECE) teacher trainer (who is also an accomplished Suzuki violin teacher), Sharon Jones, had the following to say about success:

> Successful families work together happily; they find joy in the process. They love the experience and progress at a comfortable pace.

> They figure out how to be good cheerleaders for their children. I always have the image of the face of a parent—head up—huge smile on their face while watching their child in a group class.

> Children are looking out (while playing in group class) and are seeing that parent watch them, rather than the parent's head down getting work done or on their phone, as many of us are tempted to do.

> We must not convince ourselves that children don't see this inattentiveness. Parents really have a brief opportunity to be involved. After all, we don't go to school with them and so on.

One particular student of mine, who was very successful on the instrument, comes to mind. He currently plays professionally in a major orchestra. Perhaps he didn't always practice a lot every single day during those early years, but this is one thing we can point to that he had: a great cheerleader in his mom. I believe the most successful families have this. It's not always the families that practice the most or have other advantages that are most successful, but this is definitely one thing that makes them stand apart.

Success also means hanging in there through the middle school years and everything that causes kids to stop [lessons]. It's how we focus on the bond between parent and child. SECE (Suzuki Early Childhood Education) does a good job of providing opportunities for this bond to develop in a strong but relaxed way over months and years.

## What Does That Mean for You?

I think Sharon Jones's description of families working happily together and finding joy in the process is a very important, and hugely accurate, statement. Sometimes this comes easily for families and sometimes it doesn't. Those who learn how to work together well and enjoy the process have success—on the instrument, and in all the other ways we are defining it in this book.

How do we learn to work together and to enjoy the process? How do we help our children be successful at their instrument? That is what the upcoming chapters of this book will address.

I also had the privilege of interviewing Suzuki violin teacher trainer Ronda Cole about her view of success:

Suzuki told us to first develop character. That is success!

> I always have a vision for my students. I envision them playing the Tchaikovsky Concerto, expressively with poise, confidence, and a love of sound, expression, and facility. I have faith in this vision even though this child may be sucking his thumb and sitting under my piano because Mommy left his teddy in the car. I rarely downgrade my musical expectations, but I do flex the expected pace as I see how the child learns as he matures.

> Children learn better when they know they are respected, when the people in their life are excited to see how beautifully they can learn. I love my students best when I see the courageous struggle toward the next accomplishment. I ask, "Is your brain sweating? Yes? Good for you. I knew you would hang in there until you got it!"

> Certainly learning is better and easier when there is real interest. I endeavor to spark their mindset by saying, "Isn't it interesting that . . .' or 'What do you think?"

> I find that the students who develop to be the most expressive players are ones who can identify their feelings and imagine and create multiple scenarios to support the music they are playing.

I like to feel that I am helping to develop the type of person who, as an adult, I would like to count as a friend for all the years to come. I am mindful of speaking to my students in a way that fosters their self-respect. I want them to see themselves as having resources, as a person whose joy is in supporting others, who is able to speak to others in a contributing way, or to a room full of people, without judging themselves or being afraid. At some point in their lives, they will discover that people, despite exterior differences, are more alike than they are different.

I also want to develop kindness; security; quick, retentive minds; students who take responsibility, listen to instructions, and follow them, or are comfortable asking questions if they don't understand.

Successful students support others and know everyone is on their own path working with their own frontier (rather than comparing themselves). All of this expands to make a beautiful life. Suzuki said the purpose is to make a beautiful heart. It takes a whole village to do this: including teachers and parents.

As you can see from these comments, success in this method goes way beyond just skills on the instrument. It means students don't give up when they feel like they are learning things slower than their peers. It means developing into a leader in the studio and helping mentor younger students. It's learning the discipline of working a little every day to excel at something. Success is learning to concentrate deeply. It's learning to practice and play with ease.

If I have students who have learned these things, I consider my job successful. It's not just about the instrument. It's also about who we become when we learn to play that instrument.

Suzuki parent and blogger, Alan Duncan at The Suzuki Experience, put it very well:

> I think it's all bound up in a connection between technical competence, musicianship, and character. There are a lot of pathways to technical excellence but not all build a joyful, positive, and generous attitude. Do I have a child who is growing musically, listens avidly, approaches practice happily (usually), and understands deeply from having done it thousands of times? Who knows how to approach a new challenge by breaking it into smaller, manageable steps? Do I have a child who genuinely enjoys music for its own sake? If yes, then that's a successful Suzuki experience.[3]

The Suzuki method is not just about developing professional musicians. That was not Suzuki's main goal. This method is about something bigger than that. In his book, *Nurtured by Love*, Suzuki says, "I just want to make good citizens. If a child hears good music from the day of his birth, and learns to play it himself, he develops sensitivity, discipline and endurance. He gets a beautiful heart."[4]

When we spend time daily and weekly doing the things addressed in this book, especially over a number of years, we can't help but grow as people. This can be true in many disciplines a child may undertake, but music I think has a special ability to develop great people along with great musicians, as Suzuki was inspired to do.

When I refer to success during this book, I am referring to all of this, way beyond, but including, skills on the instrument. Yes, we want to develop students and young musicians who play to the best of their abilities, but it's not only that. How do the skills we learn become part of the identity of our children and students? How does it affect who they are as people?

## Focus on a "To-Be List" Rather than a "To-Do List"

Being a Suzuki parent can feel like a big to-do list: attend lessons, take notes, ask the right questions, attend group classes and recitals, make sure your child has all the materials and equipment they need, listen every day, and practice every day. That's quite the list and most likely your teacher expects you to do it (or most of it) every week. It's an important list, there's no doubt about that.

It was this daunting list of tasks that overwhelmed me as a young mom and teacher, and I know it can feel that way to many other parents as well. I would like to suggest that yes, all of this needs to happen, but we can change the way we think of it from a list of to-dos to a list of things *to be*.

I know that when I switched my thinking as a parent from things my children need to do, over to whom I want to raise them to be, it radically changed my parenting. As a parent when I shift the focus away from all the little things I want done just right, it takes a lot of stress away.

Tasks that become habits (like brushing our teeth) are not stressful or hard to fit into our lives because we really want the outcome from doing it (be people with healthy teeth and gums). It's the end goal that motivates us and makes us do it every day.

The same thing is true with music. What is your goal for what you want your child to learn through music? That is the motivator to get the instrument out and practice, to listen to the assigned recordings again today, and to attend group class or that recital. Thinking of each part of the process can be overwhelming. I would suggest focusing on your long-term goal and making the little details into habits that are part of your day.

Be present, be a family that listens to beautiful music, be committed to daily practice, be a part of your Suzuki community, be focused on mastery and artistry, be encouraging, and be focused on the big picture.

As a teacher, I am passionate about the idea that if we focus on what we want *to be*—as a family, a parent, a teacher, or a student—then we can create an environment that helps students to be successful. Having a lot to do is stressful. Having the chance to develop into who we want to be is inspiring and motivating.

How do we keep this focus as Suzuki parents when there is so much to do? I would argue that it takes a big shift in our mindset. A whole different way of looking at what we are doing. It takes a change from seeing music lessons as just another activity on your calendar. It means letting this process influence who we are.

Fifteen years from now, it won't particularly matter that your child practiced their instrument on any given Tuesday or listened to their CD on one particular day versus another. But what will matter is the kind of person this process has developed them into. Who are we raising our children to be? Who will they become when they develop discipline, love of learning, and confidence? Who will they be if they do hard things even when they don't feel like it? Who will they be if they have parents who are present with them and strive to understand them?

Suzuki families who succeed have a mindset that allows for imperfection but focuses on the big picture. They don't get bogged down in every detail, but they know that in music, details do matter.

There are times when every day feels successful, and other times when success may not be felt at all in the day-to-day parts of the process.

Sometimes it seems a certain technique or piece has got us stuck in place and it's tempting to wonder if it's worth it to keep going or if this activity is actually a good one for us. But it's the pushing through those hard times without giving up that teaches our children something valuable.

I have seen time after time in my own teaching the feeling of accomplishment and confidence that comes from a child making their way through a tough time, or a tough piece to learn—when they stick with it and eventually come through the other side, it is such a rewarding feeling.

## Struggle and Developing Grit

As a Suzuki student myself, this kind of struggle, and then eventually overcoming the struggle, is a big part of what makes me successful today. I am not tempted to give up if things are hard. Sometimes I come up against problems that seem daunting in all areas of life, but I've learned through my study of music how to take a deep breath, step back, and look at a little piece of the problem that I can work on, and then how to chip away patiently until a little progress is made.

Writing this book is one example. I knew I had some important things I wanted to say to families I work with and the Suzuki community at large. But where to start? Once I had spent a good month writing, it became clear just how big an undertaking writing a book is. There are layers upon layers of things I didn't even realize I would need to learn. It's sort of like starting the process of learning an instrument, I think. Sometimes we can think, "Wow! This is much more involved than I realized when I decided to do this!"

But all the lessons I personally learned as a Suzuki student have supported me through this process as well. So, if I feel a little overwhelmed . . . after taking a deep breath and deciding that this is a goal worth pursuing, I moved forward each time by finding one little thing I could do to either inspire myself or improve what I was working on. Sometimes I read books about how other people write. A music equivalent might be attending a live concert or watching a famous musician on YouTube. Maybe reading an interview with a musician about when they were a student and everything was not easy, or reading a blog post from a Suzuki teacher that helps us feel like we're not alone in our struggles.

I also focused on one little thing that I could improve or work on and just got to work on that, to make it easier. The same is true if you are working on something on your instrument. Just do something every day and over time, you start to see improvements.

A great resource to read more about this process is Dr. Angela Duckworth's book, *Grit*.[5] Duckworth is a researcher at the University of Pennsylvania who studies the subject of grit, which she describes as a combination of passion and perseverance. Through her research, Duckworth has found grit to be one of the most accurate ways of predicting success, even more than IQ, test scores, and other factors that people tend to assume would equal success.

Duckworth's research on grit shows that it can be developed, especially through activities like dance, sports, and music. Not only that, but once someone has become "grittier," that characteristic carries over into other areas of life, which would come as no surprise for those who have developed this characteristic through Suzuki lessons and can attest to the many ways it helps students in other areas of life.

Because of her research on this topic, Angela Duckworth and her husband have a "Hard Thing Rule" in their house to help everyone develop grit. Everyone in the family picks at least one thing that meets that requirement, parents included. Your family is in fact doing this by being involved in Suzuki lessons.

Duckworth describes the process of her daughters developing grit in ballet class like this: "And so it was in ballet class, more than at home, that Lucy and Amanda go to rehearse developing an interest, diligently practice things they couldn't do yet, appreciate the beyond-the-self purpose of their efforts, and, when bad days eventually became good ones, acquire the hope to try, try again."

I think this sums up learning something challenging like a musical instrument very well. The diligent practice of something we can't yet do, staying consistent, and eventually seeing progress that spurs us on to try the next step in the process.

# Practical Ideas That Lead to Success

Below is a brief overview of some of the practical elements that help families succeed. I have found them to be necessary for my students to make good progress while learning to play their instrument.

# Be Present

In the Suzuki method, parents are physically present in lessons and practice sessions (at least in the early years). But, even more than being physically there, being *mentally* present and engaged in the process is an important factor for success. Parents who pay close attention to what motivates their child, how they learn, and how to accomplish the teacher's practice assignment (keeping all of that in mind) give their children a huge advantage.

As a teacher, I am always trying to figure out what will make each student stay motivated, work hard, and love music at the same time. You, as the parent, have an advantage in that you get to see and work with your child daily and will know these things so much better than the teacher does. Use this to your advantage to help your child not only with their instrument but also with anything else they wish to accomplish in life.

# Daily Practice

Making it a habit to practice daily is one of the keys to making progress on any musical instrument. Of course, every day can't be ideal and unexpected things may come up that get in the way of practicing. But there is just something about working at a skill each day and then coming back to it again and again that makes it easier over time.

Quite often, students will understand the concepts they are learning in lessons a lot sooner than they can do them with physical ease. I often talk to my own students about how they may understand a concept but their muscles need to practice and learn it as well. This can only come from the muscles having plenty of practice over time. It goes far beyond just understanding how to do it once the right way.

Coming to the instrument every day to work at a skill again and again is what gives us the ability to play our instruments well. The same progress won't be made if we only practice a few times a week. In order to be successful, daily practice is a big part of the process.

## Listening

Listening to the Suzuki recordings and other great music is another important element to success. The Suzuki method is based on the way children learn their native language. We wouldn't expect a child to become fluent in a language they were not hearing on a regular basis and we can't expect students to know how to make beautiful music on their instrument if they haven't heard beautiful music on a regular basis, either.

Listening to the Suzuki recordings means the difference between learning with ease and struggling through it. It means the difference between having a mental picture of how a piece sounds and racking one's brain for the next note. Committing to the Suzuki method means committing to listening to great music, every day if possible.

## A Positive and Supportive Musical Environment

Another part of your child's success in this method is the kind of music environment you set up for them as a parent. If your child feels that practicing with you is going to be full of positive interactions, you will encounter less resistance. I tell the families that I work with that learning to work together successfully is one of our first priorities.

Your child will be most successful if you can figure out how they learn, and approach challenges. You can help guide them through the process of working through these challenges as they come up once you know this information. This will enable you to help support your child in ways that will not only help with success on the instrument, but also in other areas of life where they will encounter similar struggles. You can help them put this knowledge about themselves to good use in order to overcome any sort of obstacles they face.

## Be a Part of the Suzuki Community

Successful Suzuki families don't just practice at home and attend lessons. They are an active part of the Suzuki community. This may mean the community in your teacher's studio, or the music school where you take lessons. It may also mean the bigger Suzuki community if you have city-wide or state events you can attend. It can mean attending Suzuki institutes (summer camps) and workshops as well. When your child is around other students who are growing and improving, it provides such a huge motivation for practice and for them to improve their own playing skills as well. Playing in a larger group is a powerful way to do this. Take advantage of every opportunity you can like this to help keep motivation strong.

## Focus on Mastery

Successful students focus on mastering their music and playing their instrument well rather than always rushing on to try new things. A new piece can feel exciting and motivating. But real progress is made on our long-term goals when we take music we already know and refine it to sound more advanced, more beautiful, and more polished.

What songs you know is far less important than how you play them. Your teacher will give you assignments to review material you've already learned and this is why. It is shortsighted to rush through this part of practice or skip it altogether. This is where we really develop our ability to play well.

## Focus on the Big Picture

Signing up for Suzuki lessons is a long-term commitment. It is not a "let's try this to see if we like it" sort of deal. It's a commitment to the process. If you decide to learn a new language, you probably won't like it through the beginning struggles of learning vocabulary and conjugations, but you will feel pride at your accomplishments along the way as you gain more skills. And that in itself is its own kind of fun.

Music is much the same: you commit to it, you struggle through learning the mechanics of how to make a sound and how to play, and eventually from all the effort put in, you start to feel a sense of accomplishment and begin to have fun playing music.

Watch other students who are further on the journey than you. Have faith you will get there. Focus on the people or future adults you are raising as parents and the things we are helping them develop in themselves through this process. There are many things in life that shape who we are as people, and music is an especially powerful one!

Now that you've had an overview of what success in the Suzuki method looks like, let's look at each of these areas more in-depth.

# The Habits
# of Successful
# Suzuki Families

Be Present | Practice Daily | Listening | Environment | Community | Mastery | Big Picture

**Be Present**

Practice Daily

Listening

Environment

Community

Mastery

Big Picture

# Be Present

**4**

*"The greatest gift you can give
your child is your presence."*

—*Alice Joy Lewis*

We live in a distracted culture and everyone, myself included, feels pulled in many directions. We all have different responsibilities pulling at us all day long. It can feel like a tall order to sit and give your child your total attention during a music lesson, and even more so to give that undivided attention during practice on a daily basis at home. However, being fully present—not just physically, but mentally and emotionally—is one of the characteristics of successful Suzuki families.

As hard as it is, there just is no substitute for being present with your child in this way. The impact it will have on their success both when learning their instrument and on how their character develops is huge. I challenge you to give your child the gift of your full attention during lesson and practice times, even when it feels really hard to do so.

# What Being Present as a Suzuki Parent Looks Like

In the beginning stages of Suzuki parenting, you will be asked to recreate your child's lesson at home. This means carefully watching what the teacher is doing in lessons and making sure your child practices those same things at home all week long.

You may need to come up with creative ways to accomplish your teacher's goals that are specific to your child, because you have the advantage of knowing your child best. You also have more days in a row to carefully observe how they learn, what helps your child learn new concepts most easily, and how to work with them the best way. Taking in all of this information and putting it into practice takes a lot of focus and observation. It simply won't happen if a parent is distracted during lessons and practice and cannot be fully present.

With young children, this means putting away electronics, finding a quiet spot in the house, and turning your full attention to your child. Notice the things that cause them to lose focus, and also notice what helps them draw out their ability to concentrate fully. This involves being creative and trying many different approaches when working with your child in practice each day until you figure out what works best.

If you find something that really works (or really doesn't work), make note of it. This is how you will know how to work with your child more successfully the next time. Notice what time of day helps your child focus best, and notice what helps keep them engaged in the process. Be a student of how your child learns. This is not only going to help with music and practice, but in every other area of life as your child grows older and you coach them how to navigate through hard things in practice, school, and beyond.

## Being Present with Teens

When your child is a teenager, being present might look a little different. It often means being available to sit in the room and be a quiet presence while they are in charge of the actual practice. By now, they likely have learned how to pay attention to detail through the way you practiced with them when they were younger.

Many teens will practice independently and be in charge of organizing their own practice sessions. Some teenagers will still practice best with their parents as a quiet presence in the room, while others will want to practice totally alone. Either way, your presence will be important at concerts and performances and as a listening ear if they want to talk about lessons or practice struggles. I can tell you from raising my own teens that they often need us, especially for emotional support, more than they will ever say. Be an enthusiastic audience, be encouraging, and be present when they do want to talk through anything. They appreciate it more than they can articulate.

## My Story

My dad was my primary practice partner growing up. I remember him sitting patiently and offering helpful suggestions when I needed it or simply being a steady presence in my practice sessions when I was dealing with frustration over learning something new. By paying close attention to what would work best when helping me, he learned what made me willing to stick it out through frustrating moments and how to best encourage me, even when my attitude could have used some improvement.

I remember especially as a teenager that my dad understood me like no one else and I have no doubt that came from all those hours of practicing together. He gave me his undivided attention every single day that we practiced together. Actually, I was very lucky that both of my parents parented this way in many parts of my life.

As a young child, I remember asking my dad to come in the living room after he got home from work one day to watch some choreographed marching I had come up with while listening to my Suzuki recording. I am sure it was nothing interesting to watch, but I can still remember him saying, "What a great way to learn your music!" and acting very interested. I am sure he was tired, and spending time practicing with me was not first on his list of relaxing activities for the evening. But he never let on that it was anything but great to spend time together practicing. His interest and presence when it was time to practice formed a strong bond between us.

Try as I might to recall the actual practicing we did together, what I remember most is how it felt to work with my dad—to feel like he was really focused on what I was doing and how much it meant to me to have him just being there while I practiced. I think being truly present was a huge gift that both of my parents gave to me.

## How to Stay Present

It's easy to get distracted with cell phones, emails, and an endless list of to-dos that have to be done as adults. It can feel stressful to take time away from what we need to do to practice with our children. But spending time really connecting one-on-one with our children is a huge gift to them and to ourselves as well.

I recommend seeing practice with your child as a rare opportunity to spend one-on-one time together. If your child thinks of practice as a series of close interactions with a parent who cares about them and enjoys spending time with them, that goes a long way toward developing a good habit and good feelings about practice.

Quality time together doing something meaningful is in short supply in our busy world. Practice, done well, is a good opportunity to do this on a regular basis. This can be a time to really get to know your child: how they learn and what kind of encouragement actually motivates them and keeps them interested.

You will get a chance to share in your child's successes when they have a breakthrough learning a difficult skill, and get to help coach them through their frustrations. It's good to ask yourself questions like: How does my child approach new problems and challenges? What do they need from me, as the parent, to succeed?

This is not just about practicing an instrument—the skills we learn during practice carry over to schoolwork and many other parts of our lives. When we empower our kids to learn new things and push through challenges, we are helping them develop important life skills. If we pay attention to what we're learning here as Suzuki parents, we will have so much more information about how to help our children understand themselves and navigate other new challenges in the future.

If you are just starting out, you are at a bit of an advantage. You can make it a habit right from the start to give your child your full attention during practice and lessons. Your practice sessions will likely be very short and you can build the habit of being present from the start in small bursts of time that are your daily practice sessions.

Suzuki violin teacher trainer (and mother) Alice Joy Lewis describes it very well below:

> The greatest gift you can give your child is your presence. For children, this is really the greatest reward: more of your time. This isn't just for music but for anything that your child needs motivation for. Being one hundred percent in tune with your child is the greatest gift you can give them. You are showing them that they are worth your time and attention. It really is a gift to yourself as well as to your child. It's a way of knowing someone that is pretty special. When parents are not distracted, the opportunity for progress to occur is great.

## Staying Present in Practice

Your child may be just starting and may only need ten or fifteen minutes of your focused time and presence during practice to get started. It's easiest to develop this good habit from the start when practices are short and then add time to the practice as your child learns more material and as their attention span increases.

If you've already started and have not been particularly paying attention to this part of your role as a Suzuki parent, it may take some work to create new habits. I would start by adjusting the way you think of and approach the practice time with your child first.

Start by challenging yourself to stay extremely focused and engaged for a few minutes to build this new habit, and then gradually extend the time you stay fully present during your child's practice sessions.

## The Parent as the Positive Environment

In SECE classes, we emphasize how important a positive environment is to learning. One of the huge shifts in thinking that I had when going through my SECE training was that for young children, it's really *the parents* who are the environment.

As the parent, you are creating the tone, the positivity, and the pace that shapes the practice environment from the start. If you ever feel that practice has taken on a negative tone, it is time to reevaluate the practice environment. Sometimes we are trying to practice during a particularly stressful time of day for us as parents, or when our child is extra tired or hungry. Looking closely at when and how we practice can help us make changes and move forward.

This is a personal topic for many parents. Don't feel bad or blame yourself if things aren't going well. But do take a long hard look at what you can change—keeping your family, your particular child, and your schedule in mind.

I know I had to work at this as a Suzuki parent myself. To be honest, it's much easier to be patient with other people's children than your own. I had to work to stay patient and relaxed every day that we practiced together. Families who take on the mindset that they will make practice as productive and positive as possible and see their role in making that happen will develop the kind of environment that helps students succeed.

It's easy to blame all bad behavior in a practice session on the child who is behaving in a less-than-ideal way. I am not suggesting that we necessarily blame ourselves as parents either, but I do think we should ask ourselves what we can do to change the tone and create a positive environment instead.

Here are some questions I recommend parents ask themselves:

1.  Is my child excited to practice together, or are they resisting it?

    Resistance to practice can come from many sources and sometimes no matter what we do as parents, our child will resist practice. It is a good idea, though, to try to take a careful look at our interactions with our children if you are seeing this reaction to practice.

2.  If they are resisting it, what do they seem to be avoiding?

    Sometimes, students are just struggling to transition from a fun activity into practice time. Other times, they are trying to avoid the struggle of working on hard things. Sometimes, they are tired or hungry or feel like practice will never end once they start. I am sure there are other answers to this as well. It may take some trial and error, but if you can figure out which of these things is causing the problem (by tweaking practice in different ways), you can often solve the problem of getting started.

3. Am I, the parent, in a positive state of mind when we start practice?

I used to make my favorite cup of coffee or tea, depending on the time of day when I practiced with my daughter, and had to really work to stay relaxed and enjoy my little treat each time, which helped me stay relaxed and enjoy it more.

4. Do I have strategies to help my child make their tasks during practice feel easier by the end?

Have a few ways to help your child accomplish the repetitions of their practice assignments that they need in order to make progress during the week. When you see frustration creeping in, have a few ways to redirect practice and keep it on track. A few examples include going back to easier review assignments, breaking the assignment into smaller parts that can be successful, and reminding your child how much easier the task will get with more practice.

5. Do I understand what motivates my child? Do I understand what will make them shut down and stop working hard?

You may have read my previous examples and thought that there was no way that would work for your child. It's great that you know that. Pay attention to what does work and what doesn't. You know your child best. Once you can approach practice with strategies you know work for your child, and avoid the ones that don't, you will see more progress start to happen.

6. Am I using this information to help create a good practice environment for my child to learn in?

It's not a bad idea to have a little list written down in the practice notebook or mentally run through a list in your head about what you know works well. There are some days when we need this kind of list more than others to help our kids have a successful practice session. Don't just observe your child; use what you observe to help them stay engaged and make progress in their practice time.

7. What can I do to help my child feel like they've had a little bit of accomplishment during the lesson today? I have noticed with the students in my studio that some leave a lesson feeling excited and motivated when we end with practicing something new. Others feel much more motivated and encouraged when we end with something easy they already know how to do well. The feeling that a student leaves a lesson or practice with tends to carry over and affect their attitude about the next session. Use this to your advantage. If we end practice feeling good about something, it truly helps.

8. What can I point out that my child is improving at, even if there are a number of things that need to be worked on?

Answering the questions above takes quite a bit of insight into your child's behavior. It is not something we can do as parents if we are only halfway paying attention. We are the child's practice environment—we have a unique opportunity to be totally present and engaged in what they are doing.

This may mean we feel frustrated or we have to deal head-on with some frustrating behaviors and help our child deal with them too. That is not easy—it is far easier to mentally check out and escape all the intense feelings sometimes. But working through that is where the biggest difference is made. Working through strong feelings is what helps give our children the tools to work through them themselves on their own as they grow older. Staying engaged through the tough practices helps us all problem-solve and learn to work together. And sometimes a nice sip of tea and a deep breath helps too.

I recently came across a great book for helping parents support students through homework struggles, and I found some of the advice very applicable to practicing an instrument too. In the book *Parent Guide to Hassle-Free Homework*, researchers from the Institute for Learning and Development shared their tips on how parents can help keep students feel engaged in their homework assignments. The list includes the following:

- challenge faulty beliefs

- give clear, consistent messages

- remind them of past successes

- give specific and positive feedback

- redefine success

- praise effort and persistence, and

- teach the importance of making mistakes and learning from them.[6]

This advice mirrors the advice I would give parents for helping students through their practice sessions. If you are unsure how to help your child practice as you are sitting with them each day, these are great places to start.

1. **Challenge faulty beliefs:** Sometimes this comes up in practice with statements from our children like: "I can't do it" or "It's too hard." Faulty beliefs like this can get in the way of progress; they cause students to stop because they don't believe they can do better.

   When our children share feelings like this in practice, I think it's important to listen and to offer another point of view so these beliefs don't become something they say to themselves every time they encounter something hard in practice or otherwise.

   Simply reassuring our children or students that the skill they are working toward is hard for everyone at first goes a long way. The false belief that a child should get something right on the first time they try is a common one. Reassure your child that this is what practice is about: taking the things that are not easy right away and making them easier over time. You might even share something with them about something you are good at now, but that wasn't easy on the first try for you.

2. **Give clear, consistent messages:** One of the authors of the book (*Parent Guide to Hassle-Free Homework*) gave the example of the children's book *The Little Engine That Could* and how the message of "I think I can, I think I

can" in the book impacted them as a child and became something they said to themselves when something was hard.

Having a similar saying that you can repeat to your child on a consistent basis is helpful. Some ideas are things like, "Keep at it—you will get it" and "You can do this." You may have a saying in your family already that can be used for this purpose. The idea is that we can change the tone of practice and how we tackle hard things when we change our faulty beliefs and replace them with new, more encouraging ones.

3. **Remind them of past successes:** Remember how hard it used to be just to hold the bow? Or to play "Twinkle"? Chances are your child has come a long way from their first lessons and pointing those things out to them when they come up against a new challenge can be very helpful. If you get stuck in practice because something is not coming easily, stopping to take stock of these things can really help.

4. **Give specific and positive feedback:** "Good job" can seem like empty praise to a child who knows they are struggling through and when they can tell something was not good yet. Instead, try to praise something specific, and truthful, that you notice. Praises like "You really focused that time" or "I like the way you did XYZ" are a lot more helpful and well received. I notice as a teacher when I do that in lessons that whatever I honestly praise, the student tends to start to do more of. It's a powerful motivation. Suzuki always said something positive to students after they played that was also honest, and it's a good practice for all of us.

5. **Redefine success:** Sometimes success in practice is not playing a piece perfectly. Often, it is good focus or concentration or a tiny improvement in one small part of a piece. If we, as parents, only define success as the former, our children are going to feel discouraged by the process.

   Success in practice can be getting in a practice session when it was a hard day to do so, or making some kind of progress so that something is better than when practice started that day, or having a good attitude for the practice session. Look at your own definition of success in practice and change it, if needed, to help your child see success in all the little steps along the way. We are all more motivated to do things daily when we can see progress. Help your child see their progress, however small, so that they stay motivated to keep going.

6. **Praise effort and persistence:** This point goes along with redefining success. At times, it's tempting to only praise correct notes or perfect posture. But what we want to develop in our children and students is a willingness to put in the best effort they can and to stick with it until it's easier. If we can get students to do these things on a regular basis, then progress on the instrument will start to happen. If we only praise the outcome but not the effort it took to get there, we're missing out on developing these great character qualities—the kind of qualities that great musicians and leaders in other fields have. I don't know any great musicians who are lazy or give up when the going gets tough—they just wouldn't develop the skills to play at a high level that way. The results will come with time. Give lots of praise about how hard your child is working and how they are sticking with hard things along the way.

7. **Teach the importance of making mistakes and learning from them:** In my experience, it is easy to confuse playing something through without mistakes with practice. If you can truly play through something with no mistakes and nothing to improve, I would argue that's not really practice. We might call it review instead.

   Real practice is taking something with mistakes and things to fix and working on it in-depth until it isn't so hard anymore. Making mistakes is part of the process of practice. Sometimes, I encounter parents who sigh loudly, make clicking noises with their tongue, or audibly say no every time their child makes a mistake while playing in the lesson. I imagine that practice goes much the same at home.

   These are often unconscious habits as parents and believe me, I have been guilty of this too. But these habits as parents are important to break. We don't want to teach our children and students that mistakes are something to fear and to avoid at all costs. In fact, sometimes mistakes are our biggest teachers. In practice, your child makes mistakes. Talk about the section you noticed isn't quite right. Ask them what they could do to fix it. Play it with many repetitions until it's easy to play correctly (this may take many practice sessions, but keep coming back to it).

   Mistakes give us information and show us where we need to work. Of course, before we perform something, we want to work out problem areas, but even then sometimes professionals make mistakes.

## Final Thoughts

These eight ways to keep students engaged and making progress in lessons are excellent reminders to us as teachers and parents alike. I would bookmark this list and keep in your practice space at home. If you're feeling discouraged or unsure of how to practice with your child, reading the list again whenever needed may help. You, being fully present, in practice with your child now and helping them learn these skills will teach them how to be fully present in their own practice one day when they are working independently. It is a huge gift to give them in order to help with their progress on the instrument, and to build a strong bond with them as a parent as well.

*"Many Olympic athletes have been cited as saying the six most important words their parents said to them were 'I love to watch you play.' Knowing your hard work matters to your parent and that you matter more than your hard work, is very powerful to a child at any age."*

—*Ann Montzka-Smelser*

Be Present

**Practice Daily**

Listening

Environment

Community

Mastery

Big Picture

# Practice Daily

5

*"Practice puts brains in your muscles."*

—*Sam Snead*

We can't talk about learning a musical instrument without talking about practice. There is no magic that happens when you attend lessons each week—it is the work you do every day in between lessons that causes progress to happen. There just isn't any substitute for the effectiveness of making time to practice every day.

Suzuki famously said: "Only practice on the days that you eat." This quote means you must practice daily to make progress, but I think given the latest research on forming habits, it means even more. Practicing daily is also smart because it is easier to follow through on set habits rather than on something we have to try hard to remember to do each day.

In Gretchen Rubin's book, *Better Than Before*, she shares her research on the different ways people make and keep habits.[7] Through her research, she discovered that keeping a habit going is much more successful when the task becomes a given part of each day and the person involved no longer has to make a decision about whether or not to do it. If you have to decide whether or not to practice each day, it can become an emotionally draining activity. This will likely cause you to skip practice some days even though you have good intentions, because it feels like a chore.

However, if practice becomes part of what your family does on a daily basis, then there is no decision to be made and the whole process becomes much simpler.

This should be our goal as Suzuki families: to think more about *when* can we practice today, not *if* we will practice today. Make it a part of your family culture to play music daily. If we're being honest, sometimes practice can feel like a chore and some days practices may need to be short, but go ahead and do it anyway.

Families who are successful long-term at the Suzuki method create this habit: they are committed to playing every day. Of course, every day can't be perfect, but if you plan to practice daily, then days without practice are an exception rather than a regular occurrence. The most successful students I work with practice five to seven days a week. Less than this, and progress will just not happen at a good pace over time.

Part of making daily practice work is scheduling time in your life to practice each day. When you make your schedule at the start of a school year, schedule in time daily for practice. If you don't have a plan and some space in your schedule for practice, it won't happen.

## Evaluate Your Own Attitudes about Practice as a Parent

In my studio, I have encountered everything from parents who are musicians and understand the importance of practice to the opposite end of the spectrum where parents hated practicing as a kid and don't want to ask their own children to practice daily. There are many families that fall somewhere along the spectrum as well.

The word *practice* can be loaded for some parents—it can bring up memories of fighting with your own parents on how to practice, or having them monitor you to make sure you used up all the minutes on the timer and aren't wasting time. It can feel constricting and unpleasant to us as adults. Sometimes, we bring a lot of baggage to the equation. I would encourage you to let that go and let your own children have a different perspective on practice. No, it's not always fun, but it doesn't have to be horrible, either. Using what we learned in the last chapter about being present and helping your child stay engaged in practice can help make their practice experience completely different from your own (if it wasn't a positive one).

If we want our kids to play a sport, we don't agonize over whether or not to send them to practices—it's just part of playing. You can't show up once a week at the game never having practiced. You won't know what to do.

It's the same thing when learning an instrument—we come to the lesson, work with our teacher, and come up with a practice plan for the week. We can't be successful in the lesson, or in group classes, if we have not done the practices during the week. Unlike some sports teams that meet twice a week, when children are young, five to seven practices gives us the best results.

Whichever attitude you are starting out with, I would encourage you to adopt the mindset of daily practice as part of daily life in your family and consider the impact this has on your child's success.

## Setting up Practice Sessions

How we structure practice sessions at home can make a big difference in how willing our children are to practice each day and how much is accomplished over the course of a week. Revisiting the assignments your teacher gave you to help your child master each day and reviewing the things that your child has already learned helps with progress, confidence, and muscle memory (which is needed for playing to become easier).

As a teacher, I would like my students to get their instrument out every day and do something. Do a complete practice session with your child every day that you can, of course, but something is better than nothing. If you only have a few minutes to practice together, it is still worth it. Play a few review pieces well or have your child play their newest piece so the new concepts your teacher is helping them improve become more automatic. Working on some technical aspect of playing for a few minutes is worth doing as well. Something is always better than nothing, and all those short sessions you would have skipped will add up to big improvements over time.

Don't be concerned about the "perfect" practice session— just get the instrument out (or sit at the piano/harp/practice singing) and do something with your child every day.

Make it a habit to play a mini concert, or to do something short when you are tempted to skip a session. If you're just starting out or have gotten out of the habit of practice, then just start with five to ten minutes but do it every day. It will get easier to add more time once you and your child are in the habit and practice is just a part of the daily routine again. If the word *practice* feels unpleasant to you, just think about *playing* every day instead.

## Practicing in Two Smaller Sessions

Depending on the age and attention span of your child, you may need to break practice up into two shorter sessions to get everything done. Some families do this with one session before school and another after school. Others do a session after school and then again after dinner.

Some of my teenage students get their practice in by breaking the practice down into multiple small chunks and doing a chunk between each school subject they are working on for homework. In the teen years, it is important to plan for practice. If we wait for an hour or a few hours to be open in our schedule so we can practice, it will never get done. This is especially true during finals or when big projects are due. Practicing scales and etudes in one chunk, review material in another, orchestra or ensemble music, and then new pieces each in their own little practice session can be very effective at this age.

It's also important for middle and high school students to learn how to plan out their practice time and how they will spend it. When students are younger, we as parents do this for them by moving on when we see that we've covered something enough for the day and to help get everything done that needs practicing. Teens need help learning to do this for themselves. Ask your teacher for help with this if it hasn't been brought up yet. Knowing how much time they realistically have and breaking down what they need to accomplish in a way that it can all get done is not only a great skill to be ready for music lessons, but it is also a great life skill in general.

Studying music can help teens learn to budget their time when they have a goal to accomplish. I've found that the teens I teach who stick with music through the high school years are the ones who use these practice chunks between subjects to relax and decompress from the other stresses of life.

Yes, practicing is work, but it uses different skills than writing a paper or studying for a test, and because it takes all of our concentration to play, it can help to disconnect from other stresses in life (at least for a short while). In my experience, when students see music as a way to relax and de-stress, then it becomes an important part of their lives that they don't want to give up, rather than just another chore to do on their long list.

## If Practice Seems like an Unpleasant Chore

I have a business coach who helped me immensely by having me ask myself, "How would this look if I made it fun and easy?" about any goal I had, but that I was having trouble making myself work on. I think it's wise to ask ourselves the same thing about practice. It is probably not possible to make every practice fun and easy, but what would it look like if it was? How do we move more toward that?

One way to do this is to make practice truly a habit in your family as we've already discussed. This at least makes the process of getting started more fun and easier. Practice will just be a given, like brushing teeth—just doing it takes less time than stalling and putting it off.

While being a co-presenter of a series of parent talks at the 2016 Oregon Suzuki Institute, my colleague Dr. Rebekah Hansen and I ran a session where parents shared their best tips for fitting practice into their daily lives.

We heard some great ideas. One family had the rule of no electronics until practice was done for the day. This approach motivated their children to get practice done for the day rather than stalling. This is something I used with my own children, particularly in the summer months when we would have long stretches of time at home and it was easy to put off practice until later in the day—and then never get it done in the end.

Another family gave their children two practice options for the day: if they picked the earlier one, then they were allowed a slightly shorter practice session. The students in this family were able to get more done and be more focused earlier in the day, and were eager to practice earlier because they knew practice would be a bit shorter.

For whatever reason, getting started is often the hardest part about practice. Getting the instrument unpacked and ready to go or simply leaving one activity that a student is engrossed in to move on to practice can be a real challenge. Setting a timer, giving lots of warning, and establishing a routine all help in getting started more easily.

Parents in my studio tell me that when their child knows that practice happens every day and that there is no convincing their mom or dad to put it off or avoid it, then they actually seem more content to do it and accept that it is part of their daily life, not a battle to fight.

## Set a Timer

Simply let your child know you are setting a timer for five or ten minutes (whichever works for you) and when it goes off, it will be time to practice. This gives students time to change gears, and hearing the timer go off is a clear signal it's time to start.

## Give Lots of Warning

Sometimes even I am engrossed in something, and although I mean to stop and go practice, it is hard to stop what I am doing and change tasks. Children can feel even more resistance to switching gears in this way.

A warning that there is just a short time left to keep doing the current activity before practice starts is far more effective than expecting a student to just drop everything at that moment and go practice. As a parent, I used this technique often to warn my children it was almost time to practice, to leave to go somewhere, or to get started on homework. We were always able to transition more easily to a new activity with some warning rather than if I insisted we change gears right away. Acknowledging that children may need this transition time helps our children feel their needs are respected and teaches children how to wrap up one activity well before moving on—something we all have to learn and carry into adulthood.

## Establishing a Routine

As a parent, I know the importance of a bedtime routine for helping prepare young children to fall asleep. When my kids were young, it often included a bath, brushing teeth, and reading a story together. It was the thing that signaled to my kids that bedtime was here and it was time to relax.

The same can be true for getting ready to practice. If we get into a routine, then fighting it becomes less of a problem and we can ease into practice as part of the routine. This will look very different for different families and depending on when you practice.

A morning practice routine could be: eat breakfast, brush your teeth, get ready to play your instrument. Or after school: come home, have a snack, get out the instrument to practice. Build a routine around practice at some point in your day.

This is the single most powerful thing I've found for helping make a smooth transition to practice on a daily basis. Often what we see as resistance to practice is really resistance to switching activities and starting something new. Understanding that this is a reality and trying to ease your child into practice will make it more pleasant for everyone.

# The Parent's Important Role in Practice

Especially when your child is young, your role as the practice parent is extremely important. Your teacher is giving you guidelines about what and how to practice, but really you are the one doing the day-to-day work with your child to get that done. Left to their own devices too early, Suzuki students will not be successful. This method depends on parental involvement, especially during daily practice sessions.

Be sure when you leave your child's lesson that you understand what to include in practice and what is the most important concept or point to focus on that week during practice. Take notes during the lesson so you can remember the small details your teacher is depending on you to follow through with all week long.

As a teacher, I always welcome questions on what to practice. I want to make sure I send students and their parents home with the right information to be successful. Paying close attention to how the teacher is having your child practice something in the lesson gives you the information you need to do that same thing at home during the week. Questions like, "How do you want us to practice this at home?" or "What's the best way to do this during practice this week?" would be very welcome in my studio.

Suzuki violin teacher trainer Ronda Cole shared with me her thoughts on the importance of Suzuki parents and their role with practicing in her studio. "Being a Suzuki parent is the most critical and also the most challenging part of the Suzuki Triangle. Suzuki parents have to be creative, be sensitive, and be ready to do whatever is needed at any time to help the maturing student. They know they have to replicate the content of the lesson at home during the week and be creative to do so."

Cole also points out that students often view the teacher's authority on what to practice differently than the parents, sometimes leading to disagreements during practice sessions. She suggests referring to lesson notes and even using the same vocabulary that your teacher does when practicing at home to cut down on this issue. Cole says, "The teacher is the teacher. The parent is the coach at home assisting the child to be ready for the next lesson."

## Wanting to Practice

Parents ask me all the time when their children will spontaneously want to practice on their own without being reminded. Many parents seem to believe that this is a sign the child really loves the instrument. I don't think the two things are related at all. I think spontaneous practice has a lot more to do with the personality of a particular child and their ability to self-start any particular activity in their lives rather than their desire to play an instrument.

My own parents had to tell me to practice all through high school. It wasn't a big fight, but they did have to remind me to get started. It wasn't that I didn't want to play violin, and later viola; I just didn't think about it myself. Looking back, I think I was not good at judging how consistent I needed to be to make good progress before my next lesson. Remember that your teenager's brain is still developing and they still need your input. I was not good at remembering to practice on my own every day, but thankfully my parents knew the importance of practice and kept reminding me.

Don't worry if you have to be the one to organize practice time or remind your child to do it. You may have to remind them all through high school to do a number of different tasks (such as cleaning their room); but we still expect them to do it and it benefits them for us to continue to ask. Hopefully at some point, your child will take ownership of starting practice on their own, and you can always reward them for practicing without a reminder as they get older to help them become motivated to start this habit by themselves.

## Changing the Practice Mindset

I think what is needed is a change in mindset about practice. Practice is not this tedious thing that we should dread. It is coming to the instrument a little bit each day in order to improve something. If something is improving—our playing, our attitude, our ability to focus and work hard— then we are being successful.

Practicing a skill daily can change who we are. It helps us develop an excitement for improving, learning perseverance, and experiencing that great feeling after you finish something that isn't easy. Learning to follow through daily and to give yourself grace to be imperfect makes a huge difference in both confidence and discipline. It's a life skill many adults struggle with. Even if your child gets nothing else out of this experience, learning this is valuable.

## Start Small

If you have to turn your whole schedule upside down to practice daily, you are unlikely to stick to it. Start with at least a short practice every day. Over time as you have more to practice and as your child's attention span grows, this will stretch out to longer practices. It is important to understand from the start that practices will extend in length the longer your child studies their instrument. You don't need to worry about it at the start, but it's something to keep in mind for scheduling in the future.

One thing I suggest to the families in my studio is that each fall, when you are planning activities, figure out how much practice is appropriate for your child's level and make sure it is in the schedule for each day of the week. Plot it out in a schedule along with the other activities your child has to see how everything fits. If you are going from one activity to another all day long without leaving time to practice as one of the activities, your child will not be successful. Success on an instrument depends on many things, and practice is a big part of that equation.

The hard reality is that if you can't find any time to schedule practice due to too many activities, then something has to go. We can't always do everything we want to all at once. Remember that we don't plan on having sports games without practices during the week and we can't plan on having successful lessons without practice during the week, either.

Even more important than the amount of time practiced each week is the amount of days practiced. There is just something about coming back to practice day after day that makes good habits and an ease of playing that cannot be found by just cramming in a couple of long practice sessions right before the lesson each week.

Doing something each day on the instrument will bring much better results. Of course, you may have days when you can practice longer and more in-depth than others. Some days our practice is going to be shorter because life happens and things come up that are beyond our control. Having a plan to practice every single day, short or long, will bring the most long-term success. It's not always easy, I know, but it is worth it.

Recently, I asked Suzuki violin teacher and parent Lisa Hansen about her daily practice habit with her own children.

> **Christine Goodner:** Why have you found it important to create a daily practice habit?

> **Lisa Hansen:** Without regular practice, progress on the violin slows and motivation dwindles for the child and parent. When I first started Zane on violin, we didn't practice daily. I gradually realized that because we didn't practice every day, his progress was minimal, as was his cooperation. Upgrading my commitment to daily practice became a game-changer, resulting in more cooperation and greater progress.

> **Christine Goodner:** What is the reality of how hard it is to make this happen?

> **Lisa Hansen:** Daily practice is not easy. It is a commitment that takes the whole family's cooperation and energy. My husband and I have agreed that daily practice is a family goal, and aligns with our values. We now have two

children playing the violin. Our basic goal is to ensure both kids spend at least one minute on the violin each day. If we set the bar that low, it is relatively easy to stick with it. The quality of the practice time is more valuable than the quantity. . . If I notice more and more protesting, it's a sign to me that something significant is going on. Tuning into the kids is vital. It might mean they need more downtime, or it might be time to implement an incentive.

**Christine Goodner**: Why do you feel like it is important anyway (despite the fact that it's not easy)?

**Lisa Hansen:** If we didn't practice every day, it would be much harder to get my kids to cooperate. Practicing is easier because it is a daily activity. Daily practicing leads to progress, and my kids are thrilled when they make it through a new piece. Success breeds success!

# Final Thoughts

As you can see, even Suzuki teachers who are parents themselves really have to work to make daily practice happen. As Lisa mentioned, being a family that practices daily doesn't have to mean you have the perfect, most thorough practice possible each of those days. It often means making a commitment to do something every day and sticking to that. It means committing to creating a family culture that includes music as a daily activity.

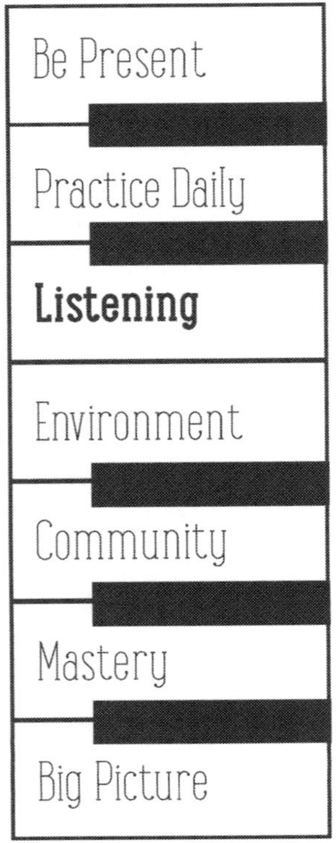

Be Present
Practice Daily
Listening
Environment
Community
Mastery
Big Picture

# Listen to Great Music

6

*"Without a doubt, the students who listen regularly to the reference recordings—and a variety of other music—are the most successful."*

*—Kelly Williamson*

The Suzuki method teaches children to play music the way they learn their native language. Think back to when your child first learned to speak. What kind of environment was around them that helped them learn to speak and understand their first language?

Likely they heard their parents, and many other people around them, speaking to them all day long. They were immersed in the language from the time they were born and they slowly, with practice, learned to understand and speak the language themselves.

Along these same lines, it is widely accepted that the best way to learn a new language, as a student or an adult, is to immerse yourself in the culture so you are surrounded by the language. In this way, new language learners learn to speak out of necessity to get around in their new surroundings.

Creating this same environment of immersion with great music can produce similar results for Suzuki students. Listening daily is one of the cornerstones of the Suzuki method for this very reason. Suzuki noticed that while he struggled to learn his second language, young children who grew up in the culture learned their native language with ease.

Many years later, we know from the field of linguistics that children's brains are taking in information and making connections based on the language they hear from birth. Listening to great music, especially on the instrument your child is studying, helps give them the same sort of information to process what music sounds like and how they want their music to sound.

One of the basic assignments you will have as a parent is to play your child's Suzuki recording for them each day. This is important for their development as a musician and will have a huge impact on how easily they will learn to play their instrument well.

Students I teach who listen to their Suzuki recordings regularly learn at least twice as fast as the students who do not do enough listening. When a student is struggling to make progress, this is the first question I ask. How much are you listening to each week?

Students who listen enough have a clear picture in their heads of how the piece they are learning sounds. They can sing or hum the tune to the next section at any given point. They also have a clear picture of what a good sound is for their particular instrument and understand when further work is needed to improve it.

This inner knowledge makes learning new music so much easier and cuts back on frustration. Make listening on a daily basis a habit in your home from the start so your child can have this advantage for learning music easily.

## Make Listening a Priority

I hear from many families that it feels hard to fit listening in daily, or that it's easy to forget to do it. As a parent myself, I understand there is a lot to fit into each day of your family's life already. However, just realizing how important this habit is to your child's success should help make this task a priority.

Besides practicing each day, *this is the most important thing* you can do. In fact, I would argue that it may be even more important than practice on any given day. Listening gives students motivation and a goal that can spur them on to practice and make learning feel more effortless. On the practice charts that my students take home with them from lessons each week, this task is on top of the list because I want them to see it as a top priority.

My colleague Lauren Lamont agrees: "Getting parents and students to listen to the recordings is sometimes difficult, but it improves their learning by one hundred ten percent!" She recommends fitting listening in whenever possible and to come up with listening games like listening for a specific note your child may recognize to keep them engaged.

## Passive Listening versus Active Listening

When you first start lessons, it is likely that most of the listening your child is asked to do will be passive listening.

That is, listening to the music as it plays in the background while your child is doing other things. For example, listening while playing, eating, riding in the car, doing homework, or any other everyday activity you can think of.

The music can just be playing on a low volume so there is no need to sit and just listen with total attention.

As your child advances, they will likely be given more active listening assignments. For example, pulling out the sheet music for a piece they are working on and following along with the printed notes while they listen. Or, listening to a few different recordings of the same piece by multiple performers to hear all the different ways a piece can be played.

There are some things you can do to make listening more active even for beginning students. Creative movement, drawing pictures of what the music makes a child think of, and making up a story to go along with the music (or even lyrics) are great ways to get students to listen carefully and notice the style, speed, and mood of pieces they are listening to.

Parent Jo-Anne Steggall has a great example of this: "Our youngest loves dinosaurs. She makes up her own lyrics to the recordings that all involve dinosaurs. It is so much easier to remember how it goes when she can sing some words that are meaningful to her."

I shared in an earlier chapter that I used to march around the room to my Suzuki recordings as a child. Some of my students have come to lessons having made up their own song lyrics to a new piece they are learning. The ideas could go on and on. Use your creativity and your child's interest to come up with ideas that work for you.

## The Bigger Picture

If we want to learn anything new as adults, it is a good practice to find people who have already done it and to learn from them. That is the principle we are teaching our children as part of the bigger picture when we listen every day. Not only does listening teach students how their pieces sound and how their instrument, when played well, sounds, but it also teaches them to seek out someone who has learned something well before them to understand how it is done. We do this as adults by finding a personal trainer if we want to get in shape, or watching a video online, or reading a book or how-to guide. We don't expect ourselves to learn how to do something without some guidance.

Your teacher will give you guidance at your lesson each week, but it takes daily guidance to do what we are talking about. Remember our language learning analogy: we won't become fluent in a language we only hear modeled once a week.

## My Own Children

I knew my own children were true Suzuki kids when I watched their approach to musical theater in high school. As soon as the musical was announced for the next school year, they would go find the music. They went straight to the library (or online), got the music, and started listening to it over and over until the whole family could sing it—long before auditions ever took place.

I didn't have to prompt them or suggest it. They knew this is how you easily learn new music: listen, listen, listen. It didn't feel like a chore; they were excited to do it so they were prepared when auditions rolled around. Once the show started, it wasn't stressful for them to learn any lyrics or music because they had listened so much. It was already ingrained in them by the time rehearsals started.

## Practical Ideas for Fitting in Listening

So exactly how do families fit in their daily listening habit?

- Play the CD in the morning as children are getting ready for the day.

- Play it in the car as you are driving to and from various activities throughout the week.

- Play it at night as your children are falling asleep.

- Use it as a soundtrack while doing other activities like playing or reading.

- I heard about one family that required it as the background listening any time their child played video games, which is a great idea!

These days, our music can be easily put on our phones and other devices to be taken with us wherever we go. This is such an advantage. When I was young, we only had the Suzuki recording on a record player in my parents' bedroom so I would hang out with them there at night to listen. We did it, but it sure wasn't convenient like it can be today.

The families in my studio often have success if they have the habit of hitting play at the same time as another activity that happens each day, and is already an established routine. If you go to the kitchen to make breakfast and hit play each time, or every time dinner is being prepped the music comes on, it actually becomes hard to forget to do it. Find what activity you can group listening up with that works best for your family and make it a habit by doing it every day. Eventually, you won't even have to think about it or remember to do it. It will become automatic, which is the best way to ensure it gets done. If listening is piggybacked on another activity, it is easy to make it a habit long-term.

## As Children Get Older

The goal is that when our kids become teenagers, perhaps late teens, they will see the power of listening for themselves and will do this without prompting. It *does* usually happen for my students at some point. Over time, students start to realize how much easier it is to learn new music if they have listened to it first. Then they will start to be the ones driven to do the listening assignments themselves. I would recommend that you see it as a parent-driven activity until that happens.

## "Listen like a Maniac"

One of the best illustrations I've heard about the power of listening was given by Michele Monahan Horner, author of the book *Life Lens: Seeing Your Children in Color*.[8] Horner gave a parent education talk through the Suzuki Association of the America's *Parents as Partners* video series called "*Listen Like a Maniac.*" In it, she shared the wildly successful experiment she did as a Suzuki teacher and parent who radically changed listening for her students and her own child.

Here is how it worked: a CD was made (you could also make a digital playlist on whichever program you use to organize your music) that included the student's newest piece and the next two pieces they were going to learn. Each song was on the CD ten times in a row. This CD, or playlist, was then assigned to be listened to every day. Michele shared the amazing results she got with this approach, which took a few students who were struggling to make progress and started giving them rapid results in their ability to learn new music well.

## Live Music

Beyond listening to recorded music at home, I highly recommend getting out to see live music in person as much as possible. Many communities have inexpensive or free concerts for children. You may find some local high school, college, or community orchestras to see at an affordable cost. It is worth the money to go see soloists on your child's instrument when your budget allows as well.

There really is something about seeing musicians perform live that is so motivating and exciting. Even as a music teacher, I often leave such concerts motivated to come home and practice. So attend as many concerts as you can.

Often students will hear something in a concert—like a certain style of music or a piece by a certain composer—that gets them excited to keep practicing so they can play it someday. This is not the kind of motivation you can get by just attending lessons. Seeing someone play and wanting to be capable of playing like them is a powerful motivator for any musician.

## Videos

If you look on YouTube, you can find many videos of professional musicians performing, enabling you to watch right in the comfort of your home. While it's not the same as seeing a performance in person, this can allow you and your child access to see musicians who may never come to your hometown, but who are very inspiring to watch. Find some of your favorite artists and follow them on social media where you can often see videos posted, information on concerts, and more information about their newest projects. I still remember seeing videos of Itzhak Perlman when I was a child and how much he inspired me and motivated me to play violin.

## Listening to Create a Mental Roadmap

One of the powerful things that happens when a student listens enough to a piece they are learning on the recording, their brain starts to form a clear picture of what comes next in the piece. This helps alleviate the struggle of learning the form of the piece, or how the pieces fit together. It takes out the guesswork and makes learning easier.

As a teacher, the difference between teaching someone who has listened enough and someone who has no clear idea of how a piece should go is night and day. There is a dramatic difference for beginners that becomes even more apparent as students progress in the repertoire. It always pains me to see a student struggle when I know the solution is often as simple as more listening. I do understand that it is not always easy to form this habit, but it is such a simple way to make learning easy that it can't be emphasized enough.

There are parts of learning a piece like the style, the mood, and what the piece sounds like when it is in tune that take a long time to explain one by one to students. Everything has to be broken down into small, incremental steps. If the student already understands these details through their listening assignments, then they already have a basic understanding of how these things happen in their piece, and we can just work on how to play the music well instead.

Parent and Suzuki teacher Jody Morrissette shared that her children light up when they begin a new piece and realize that they recognize the song already (from the recordings) and know what to expect. I have found the same to be true for students I work with.

Another teacher shared with me that younger siblings in her studio will often say they have already learned a piece they've heard a sibling play. They haven't actually learned how to play the piece on their instrument, but they feel they know it because of how much listening they have done. I can certainly say from experience that these siblings also tend to learn more easily because they understand how the piece goes inside and out.

I would state my recommendation for regular listening this strongly: to not listen enough to the recordings is to handicap a student and make it hard for them to be successful. I know it can feel like a chore to listen every day, but the effort it takes to make this happen daily is worth it!

# Final Thoughts

The Suzuki method teaches very young students to play their instruments using the same principles by which they learned their native language. A huge part of being successful at this is knowing how a piece, or instrument, should sound in the first place.

Focus on becoming a family that listens to great music as part of your family culture. You have the opportunity to have a huge impact on your child's ability to progress and feel confident learning new music by making sure this simple activity happens. Classical music doesn't have to be your own favorite genre to listen to, but you can likely learn to appreciate it as you see all the effort your child puts into learning how to play their instrument.

One of the saddest things to me was a former student of mine whose parents rarely came to recitals, did not enjoy listening to her practice, and didn't want any classical music played in the house because they didn't like listening to it. The fact was, their daughter was really passionate about it—it was part of who she was. What kind of message does this send to a child?

Embrace the journey your child is on and who they are becoming through studying an instrument. Chances are if you listen to many different performers and styles, you will find one you can connect to as a parent and your child will certainly benefit from all the exposure to great music.

I think Suzuki flute teacher trainer Kelly Williamson sums up the importance of listening very well: "Without a doubt, the students who listen regularly to the reference recordings—and a variety of other music—are the most successful. They learn their pieces more quickly and more easily. They play with better intonation. They play with more expression and better phrasing; on the flute, even the quality of their articulation is affected because students who listen are thinking in lines, instead of note by note. They are motivated to learn future repertoire pieces because they have been looking forward to learning them for a long time. The students who do the best of all are the ones who, in addition to the above, are regularly taken to live performances by their parents. One of my students came to an orchestra concert the other day and had her picture taken with me right afterward in the concert hall—as her mom clicked the camera, I was conscious that this kind of experience is part of the 'glue' that helps to hold the whole vision together, and helps my student to see herself as a present and future musician."

*"The students who do the best of all are the ones who, in addition to the above, are regularly taken to live performances by their parents. One of my students came to an orchestra concert the other day and had her picture taken with me right afterwards in the concert hall - as her mom clicked the camera, I was conscious that this kind of experience is part of the "glue" that helps to hold the whole vision together, and helps my student to see herself as a present and future musician."*

—*Kelly Williamson*

Be Present | Practice Daily | Listening | **Environment** | Community | Mastery | Big Picture

# Create a Positive, Musical Environment

7

*"Suzuki's idea was that as important as music is, the child is more important."*

—*Alice Joy Lewis*

As a Suzuki parent, you will spend time every day helping your child practice their instrument. Beyond knowing what to practice, it's important to pay attention to the kind of environment children practice best in. If your child feels like practicing with you is going to be full of positive interactions (being understanding and supportive), you will have a much easier time getting them to do it. This is the kind of environment that supports students' growth both as musicians and as great people.

When practice environments come up for discussion, I usually hear lots of physical descriptions. For example, it's a good idea to find a spot in the house that will always be used for practice and that is free of distractions and extra noise. It is also important to have all of your materials ready for practice before you start to avoid wasting time. These are important pieces of advice, but I encourage you to think of the practice environment as something else completely: *you, the parent, are the practice environment.*

I first heard about this concept through my SECE training with Sharon Jones. It is a huge shift in perspective from the way teachers and parents usually think about practice environments, but it is such an important distinction to make. You are your child's environment. A supportive and involved Suzuki parent makes a huge difference in their child's success, and not just in the results related to music.

I know it is a big job to come to lessons, get a good grasp of what needs to be practiced during the week, and then facilitate those practices at home all week long. The parents who make this work the best do it in a way that is positive and works with their children's strengths. They nurture their child through the process, helping them grow and improve along the way. To be able to do this well, it all starts with confidence in the fact that your child *can* learn to play their instrument well.

When I asked violin teacher trainer Alice Joy Lewis about the mindset of families who succeed in her program, she had this to say:

"They absolutely believe that their child will be able to learn. They absolutely have to believe that! There will be so many hills to climb, and of course wonderful spaces too. Take ownership of the fact that your child can. If you believe they can, it will happen."

This kind of belief that your child *can learn* the instrument will change the way you practice, what you expect from your child, and your patience level. It is an essential part of setting up a positive, encouraging environment for practice. The way you talk to, interact with, and react to your child sends them this message: they can do it, and will get it with practice and time.

Suzuki teacher Danette Schuh says that this belief that your child can learn reminds her of the Henry Ford quote: "'Whether you think you can, or think you can't—you're right.' Sometimes parents can stress out about how their child is progressing," she says, and this is what she tells them: "I wouldn't worry about minor setbacks . . . Progress tends to bounce around and if you could graph it on a chart, it wouldn't look like a nice smooth incline, but probably more like the Rocky Mountains! With long-term perseverance, students always end up getting there."

As teachers, we often have enough experience with students to know and trust that students end up getting there. We know that everyone may go their own speed and have their own challenges, but over time, they will do fine if they practice and continue to learn.

As a parent, you may only see your own child's progress and it may be hard to gauge how things are going. It is important to trust your teacher and to remember that no matter how fast or slow progress is going at the moment, it is worth sticking with it.

There will be times when your child makes great progress and other times when it is hard to tell if anything is happening. Your understanding and encouragement can make the difference between continuing and learning that hard things take time and effort or getting discouraged and giving up.

As Suzuki parents, sometimes the biggest part of our job is to encourage our children. It's important to let them know that while it is hard to play an instrument, they absolutely can do it with effort and practice.

When I work with students in my own studio, I often find that just hearing from me (or a parent) that a task or skill is hard for everyone at first, and that it just takes practice to make it easy, is all a child needs to hear to keep working. If we believe they can do it, they will likely adopt the same attitude.

## Staying Positive

Practice can bring up strong emotions. It often involves striving toward a goal that does not come easily. Depending on the student, this can bring up a lot of feelings of frustration. As parents, we need to be committed to setting a tone of encouragement and building up our children. Focusing on what is going well, no matter how small it seems, can help. Remember that nurturing our children as people, not just musicians, is one of our main goals.

Some parents may spend a good amount of time helping their children work through feelings of frustration. Remember that we want to create a positive and nurturing environment for our children to learn in, including learning to work through these sorts of feelings. Be sure to talk with your teacher if you are struggling with this.

Here are some productive ways to help keep a practice positive when a student is frustrated:

- Ask the student to tell you what the teacher wants them to work on. This way, they are thinking for themselves rather than being told what to do. This helps develop ownership and helps the student feel like they are working toward a goal that they are a part of.

- Pick only one point to work on with each assignment and stick to it as a parent (no matter how many other things you'd like to address).

- Emphasize the positive. In some extreme situations, parents may work out a system with the teacher where they only mention positive things seen in practice and leave the constructive criticism to the teacher.

- Remind your child of other times they have found something hard and how it has become easy because they have practiced. This can be something to do with their instrument or any other skill they have developed.

- Spend a lot of time each practice doing things your child can do well, rather than only challenging assignments. If a particular assignment is frustrating them, take a break with an easy task on the instrument, and then come back later or another day to work on it again.

- Try to end each practice with something fun and enjoyable, such as a favorite piece or game. The feeling your child leaves practice with will stick with them. End on a positive note.

- Keep feedback about what to practice non-personal. "Your thumb is wandering away from its spot" is much easier to hear as a student than "You forgot to bend your thumb." Playing an instrument is a deeply personal thing. Build up your child as a person while you discuss an issue that needs improvement.

Many students enjoy performing and playing in groups but find individual practice a frustrating experience. Helping them focus on the parts they love playing can help with motivation. Remember this process is a long-term commitment. There will be ups and downs along the way. It is easy to confuse frustration with not learning a technique or song easily with not liking the instrument as a whole. Over time, we can help our children see the difference.

## Be Realistic about What You Can Accomplish at Each Practice

There is nothing that kills positivity and causes frustration in a practice session like having unrealistic expectations of what your child can accomplish. Young children can only realistically focus on one thing at a time. If you ask them to focus on their posture, hand position, and tone, something will suffer.

As adults, that is sometimes hard to relate to and easy to forget. You can figure out what is a reasonable expectation by watching how your teacher works with your child and observing your child as they practice at home.

In his book, *The Talent Code*, Daniel Coyle explains three zones of learning that I think can really help us think about this.[9] First, there is the "the comfort zone": this is where everything is relatively easy to do.

The opposite extreme is what Coyle calls "the survival zone," where there is too much struggle. Students who are trying to practice in this zone often only successfully complete what we're asking them to do half of the time or less. It's a good signal to us as parents if our children are trying to practice and are in this zone to break things down into smaller pieces to help them be successful.

Coyle's research shows that the most progress is made in "the sweet spot." This is where students are striving with everything they have to get something correct and can just barely do it. In this zone, they probably can do correct repetitions about 70 to 80 percent of the time. But when the task is new, they are really reaching and giving it all they've got to that much accuracy. Coyle says that students who practice in this zone can make more progress in five to ten minutes of practicing this way than in months of practicing in the comfort zone.

Great teachers have really perfected the art of finding that "sweet spot" for their students to work in and helping their students strive just enough to keep making progress without it feeling impossibly hard. As parents, we can strive to do the same with our children at home during practice.

Playing scales and review pieces may fall into the comfort zone as they become easy to play but when working on something new, we can strive to find a balance of striving to improve but not making things so hard our children cannot achieve them.

Being realistic about what can be accomplished in each practice session (or at one time) can help keep practice more positive and help avoid frustration. You can only do so much in one sitting and that's why it's important to come back to it day after day to build on what we've already done. Over time, your child will be able to play music you never imagined if you keep up this approach.

Learning a musical instrument is more of a marathon than a sprint. If we tire ourselves out or frustrate ourselves by expecting to accomplish things more quickly and easily than is possible, we are not helping ourselves in the long run. It is hard to stay motivated if we feel like the whole process is frustrating and unproductive. That is what tends to happen when our expectations are unrealistic.

One key I have found to avoiding frustration as a parent and as a teacher is just to take each child as they are, that day, and help them improve from there. Focusing on where we think their progress should be or on the fact that something was easier last week is not helpful or encouraging to anyone. Look at the child in front of you—see where they are today and help them make things a little easier and gain a little more confidence. Sometimes, it may feel like we go three steps forward and then two steps back. Be encouraging anyway. Sometimes it will feel like you are coasting downhill and things are coming easily, but still be encouraging (and enjoy it while it lasts).

## Setting the Tone for Practice

As the practice parent, you have a powerful role in setting the tone that practice sessions will take. This takes an effort on your part to be very intentional with how practice happens. Despite the other things that are stressing us out as adults, or how our child may have acted in another situation earlier in the day, we can start fresh each practice session.

I suggest taking an approach of working together with your child to make practice productive. Avoid practice battles or power struggles over what to practice. If you are having trouble making this work, please talk to your teacher. I always want to know if a family is struggling with this so that I can help brainstorm ideas.

Focus on the positive. A big part of your job is to try to give your child the tools to learn to work through challenges, ideally as positively as possible.

Before your child is old enough and competent enough to practice on their own, you will be a big part of the process. What we say to them now when things are hard and when we don't want them to give up often shapes what they will say to themselves later. Some parents even write down ideas of how to say something in a way that builds up and encourages their child, rather than vents their own frustration so that they have some ideas before practice happens.

## Things to Encourage

Sometimes all we can see are the many things our children still need to work on. What do we say that is positive and encouraging when we see so much that does not look positive to us? I would encourage you to focus on the traits your child is developing through practice.

- Encourage focus.

- Encourage hard work.

- Encourage sticking to things when they are not easy.

- Encourage careful listening and noticing small details.

- Encourage a beautiful sound.

- Encourage trying even if you might not be successful.

- Encourage the willingness to come to practice with a good attitude.

Whether you are encouraging musical skills or character qualities, be careful of false praise. Children can tell if they sound good or not, especially with all of the listening they do. Telling a child something sounds great, when it really doesn't, is false praise and in my experience, children see right through this. If you find something true to say, it is much more effective.

It could be as simple as saying, "I think that was the best one!" or "It looks like it's getting easier!" At first, it may be hard to notice all the tiny details that are going well. As a parent, it's a good habit to get into as our children are growing up and as children, it is good to have them notice these tiny baby steps as well.

## Know How Your Child Learns Best

There are many ways to approach the same task. Playing something twenty times feels like work. Finding out how your child best learns and is receptive to practicing can make practice both more effective and more fun. A critical part of creating a positive practice environment is learning how your child feels most willing to work hard on a new skill.

Some students think it's fun to check off boxes for each thing they have practiced.

Other students love games like moving a small toy from one end of the table to the other after each repetition.

Some students think it's fun to draw pieces of paper out of a bowl to decide what to practice next so they are directing the order of practice.

Others think it's fun to know that practice always goes in the same order and they can depend on the routine.

Knowing what motivates your child and integrating that knowledge into practice goes a long way toward productive and positive practice sessions. If your student really dislikes practice games, putting them into practice sessions will not be helpful.

There are some great resources for identifying how your child works best. The DISC profile, using the *Life Lens: Seeing Your Children in Living Color* book, and many others. They all have different ways of categorizing the patterns we see in how our children and students learn and approach new things. I think they can all be simplified in the following way to get a clearer picture of what helps your child learn best.

In my experience, students tend to fall into these practice styles:

- Self-directed

- Parent/adult-directed

- Game-oriented

- Detail/checklist-oriented

Many students will be some combination of these four categories, but the following descriptions will give a basic way of understanding how your child may practice best.

**Self-directed:** These students like to feel in control of how practice will go. They are happiest and most willing to work hard when they can pick what they are working on. These are students who may benefit from rolling dice to see how many times they are to play something. They respond better to drawing the name of a piece out of a bowl or reading it on a list than being told by their practice parent. Giving them lots of choices between two acceptable options often works well too.

**Parent-directed:** In contrast to the last group, students who prefer this type of practice like having practice structured by an adult. It may be as simple as going through your notes from lessons or your practice sheet and helping your child move from one activity to another with verbal cues. These students might not feel comfortable directing their own practice and feel perfectly comfortable having you set the agenda for them. I think the important thing to help practice go smoothly is to have your own plan of action before you begin practicing.

**Game-oriented:** It surprises some parents that not all students are game-oriented in practice. Some students will act insulted at the idea of playing a game during lessons while others love it! You can find endless practice game ideas online.

Here are a few ideas:

- Little items to count for repetitions like cute erasers, craft pom poms, coins, or anything else you can come up with.

- Blank game boards that you can write practice assignments onto: you can use small toys as game pieces and roll dice to move around the board.

- Card games made out of index cards: list items to be practiced (one per card) and have your child draw one at a time at random.

- Roll dice or use a game spinner to determine the number of times to practice a section assigned by the teacher.

- Fishbowl: Write all the items to be practiced that day onto slips of paper and put them in a bowl or bucket. The student pulls them out one at a time to see what to practice next.

It is smart to have a few games in mind before practicing and to change them every so often, as usually a new game can bring some fresh energy into practice.

**Detail/checklist-oriented:** Some students really love having a practice chart. They may check off boxes after each item practiced, add stickers, or simply enjoy going down the list to get everything accomplished. A sure way to frustrate a student like this is to not have a practice plan or way to mark off that a task is completed. If your teacher does not give you a practice chart to check off, you can come up with your own or even find colorful blank charts at school supply stores that can be used to mark off successful completions.

Over time as you practice with your child, you will begin to see patterns of how they learn and will probably be able to tell which category (or categories) they fall into. If you use the framework above to think about what you are seeing, you will likely have a better idea how to make practice more enjoyable and productive for your particular child.

## The Importance of Environment

As a parent, it can feel like all this is nice, but that it takes a lot of time and effort. Wouldn't it be faster to just run through the assignment list the teacher gives and not worry about all of this? Maybe . . . but we are not trying to make efficient practice robots. We are trying to make an environment in which your child can learn and be successful.

When I asked Suzuki parents and teachers what the benefits of a positive, nurturing environment was for students, there were some common themes to the answers I received.

**Effort and cooperation:** Students who practice in a positive environment are willing to try harder and keep practicing because they feel encouraged. "My daughter is much more willing to put in effort when she is having fun. The more it feels like work, the more disengaged she becomes. Keeping it light and positive makes for more cooperation and ultimately more progress," says Suzuki parent Alan Duncan.

**Building a working relationship with your child:** "A positive, encouraging environment goes a long way to build trust that you are there to be an encouraging guild in their musical development," says Jody Morrissette, Suzuki parent and teacher.

**Feeling safe to try hard things:** If we feel that we are going to encounter harsh feedback or negative emotions, the tendency is to hold back and play it safe. In music, we are going to have to try new things and make mistakes in order to be successful. It is part of the process. Create an environment where your child is able to do this with you. Namrata Sharma is the parent of a five-year-old violin student who says that creating a positive environment helps her child feel safe to make mistakes and that her daughter is more willing to practice when it is fun.

## Final Thoughts

You are your child's environment. You help set the tone for practice. You will gain a special knowledge and insight into how your child learns and how they are motivated by working with them each day with this in mind.

Think ahead fifteen or twenty years: Who do you hope your child will be? How do you hope they will approach challenges they face and interesting projects they are involved in? How do you want them to look back at all those hours they spent with you practicing?

Violin teacher trainer Ann Montzka-Smelser says it well: "They focus on the child's confidence, expression, and comprehension rather than 'not making any mistakes.' Focusing on character before skill. Parents create a successful environment of support, hard work, discipline, and safety to try new challenges and make mistakes. Parents need to give this to themselves to be the best example to their children."

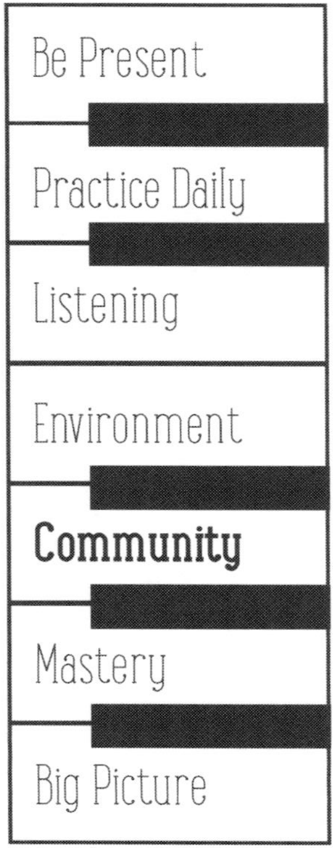
Be Present
Practice Daily
Listening
Environment
Community
Mastery
Big Picture

# Be a Part of Your Suzuki Community

*"Creating community is one of Suzuki's many great accomplishments."*

*—Alice Joy Lewis*

Successful Suzuki families know there is more to the process of learning an instrument than practicing at home and attending lessons. Part of the power of this method is that you are not in it alone—you are part of a whole community of teachers, parents, and students working toward common goals.

When we are only focused on our own journey, we can miss the bigger picture. We can forget that we are part of a bigger movement of families and parents and students who are all working to make great music, learn to do hard things, and grow as people.

Attending events in your community—like recitals, group classes, institutes, and performances—is often what inspires and motivates students to practice and keep learning their instrument. Beyond your immediate community (your teacher's studio), there will often be opportunities to participate in state or regional workshops and institutes. Take advantage of opportunities like this every chance you get. Being around people who are inspiring and on the same journey with us is so important!

Suzuki flute teacher trainer Kelly Williamson states it very well: "The most successful Suzuki families are those who commit to what I think of as 'the whole enchilada!' This includes group classes, studio recitals, community concerts, workshops, institutes, eventually chamber ensembles, and/or youth orchestra. Each of these activities builds a child's confidence with so many repeated positive experiences, applied layer by layer, that they find themselves in a cycle of being ready, prepared, and then successful."

## Group Classes

Attending group classes (if your teacher or community offers them) is a critical part of learning in the Suzuki method. In private lessons, we work on our individual playing skills, but group classes help us learn to play in ensembles. Especially as a violin teacher, there are many skills that I teach in group class that I just can't teach in the same way in private lessons alone.

As a teacher, group classes are equally important to me for teaching skills and for maintaining motivation. I want my students to come to group class because they will learn ensemble playing skills and because playing with their peers will often be the thing that keeps them practicing because they want to be ready for the next group class. It's a wonderful cycle of motivation and reinforcement of what we are practicing individually.

I often hear at lessons how a certain piece heard in group class made a student excited about practice because they want to improve enough to play it. Suddenly, a child who may be reluctant to practice has a reason to work hard and make progress. This is instant motivation and takes no effort except showing up at group class so that those moments of inspiration happen.

Group classes also give the opportunity for students to learn to play together well. Having pieces to perform as a group at recital gives us motivation to keep those pieces at a high playing level, all year long, which is no easy task.

Our studio often gets asked to play in the community: at farmers markets, retirement homes, and by the Salvation Army bell around the holidays. Once a year, the advanced group class gets to play in the lobby of the concert hall before an Oregon Symphony concert—a favorite with all of the students. The fact that we play together on a regular basis means we can be ready to perform when we are asked. Then we have the opportunity to impact our larger, non-music community as well.

Group class is also where parents connect with one another. Meeting the other parents in the studio and seeing them on a regular basis through group helps build that vital Suzuki community where parents can find support and see that they are not alone.

Violin teacher trainer Ann Montzka-Smelser shared the following about how important group classes are: "The students (and parents) who do not come to group regularly have a much higher percentage of quitting. Group lesson is a commitment; there is an accountability to the team. Friendships between parents are just as important as friendships between students. We come together to be inspired and to know others struggle too. Dr. Suzuki wanted to have all levels combined in group settings so that young students can see what their future holds and more advanced students can mentor and lead the newer students. This holds true for new and veteran Suzuki parents as well. Everyone grows."

## Recitals and Other Performances

Recitals are great motivators for practice; when there is an event to practice toward, I always see a bigger commitment to good, quality practice in my studio. Not only are performances good motivators to practice diligently, but they also provide another great opportunity to connect with other students socially and experience community. Hearing other students play and share our music with an audience are both so valuable to developing musicians. I find that parents get excited to see each other's children and compliment them on their playing and progress. A supportive and encouraging culture is developed.

## Community Experiences Are Encouraging

If you're new to the Suzuki method, it can be very encouraging to see lots of other students moving along at their own pace, just as your child is. It truly doesn't matter how fast you progress through the music; it matters if you are developing a beautiful sound, learning new things, and sticking with the process of learning an instrument. It can be reassuring to hear that other families are working hard on these same things. It's also reassuring that no one finds learning an instrument easy right away. We're all working toward the same basic goals, all at our own speeds.

This is one of the ways that community can be the most powerful: parents sharing their struggles and encouraging each other with their experiences of how they make things work with their children.

Connect with other parents when you are at community events and ask what helps them make progress the most. Find out what it was like for them when their child started and what they have learned along the way. Parents are often surprised to find out that students who look like everything is easy for them now have also struggled too.

You may see a very poised end of Book Three student performing easily, but what you don't know is that the first year of lessons were spent rolling around on the ground and not making fast progress at all. Or you may see a very polite student who is on their best behavior at recitals and performs well; but what you can't see is that they struggle to get through practice sessions without frustration.

Try not to compare what you see from other families and students in their best moments to your family and child in your worst moments. In a supportive community, we can acknowledge both that students have made great progress and that everyone is working to improve something and support each other through the process.

## Social Motivation

Besides all of the educational reasons for being part of a music community, the reality is that it's fun to play with other people. When I was a teenager, making music with my friends was the thing that kept me playing my instrument.

My motivation to practice by myself may have had its highs and lows, but I certainly didn't want to miss out on time with my music friends. Playing in a community of peers and sharing what we've learned is great social motivation.

"We're all social beings to one extent or another," says Suzuki parent Alan Duncan. "There's a phenomenon of 'social facilitation'—in a variety of pursuits, people tend to perform better in social situations. Children are also proud of what they are learning. They want to share it."

There are many things pulling for the time and attention of our children, especially teenagers, and they are less likely to keep playing if all that means is practicing alone in their room for a lesson the next week.

When students get to know each other well and make friends in the studio, it motivates them to practice for group events so they can attend. Students are motivated by the opportunity to see people they know and like.

This kind of social motivation makes teens much more likely to keep playing through the busy high school years. You may think your child doesn't have time for this sort of activity, but don't underestimate the power it has to keep them playing. I would argue they don't have time not to. Even if it's a summer camp experience or a friend to get together with once a month to play duets, find a way to get your child involved with their peers.

Being part of a community is a powerful way to keep students engaged. I would recommend any student in middle and high school to be part of some musical group even beyond their group classes with their teacher or studio. Whether it's forming a quartet, joining a local orchestra, or simply finding a couple of friends to play duets with on a regular basis. This will keep students playing during a very social and busy time of life.

## Children Learn from One Another

I am very proud to teach SECE classes a few days a week. One of the main tenets of the class is: *children learn from one another.* I have seen how true this is both in these classes and in my studio as a whole. I think teachers and parents alike can learn something from acknowledging and building on this truth about children and their development.

When younger students see their older and more experienced peers performing a task, they can see physical evidence that it is possible for them to do the task as well. They often look up to the older, more experienced students in class and work hard to imitate them.

The other side of this great relationship is that the more experienced students get the opportunity to be leaders— to show the younger students what to do by modeling and being given leadership opportunities. They get to feel celebrated because of what they have learned, which motivates the younger students to strive to reach new goals. In this way, the two groups continually feed off of each other with motivation.

This same thing happens in instrumental group classes (and other community building events) as well. Beginners see older students playing something they wish they could play, and become motivated to keep working and keep practicing.

More experienced students know they are in a leadership role and often rise to the occasion by being extra careful how they play and by showing how things are done correctly.

This kind of peer interaction benefits everyone and is a great reason to get students of different levels together to play. Even if your child or student plays an instrument that is harder to play in groups (like piano), playing for each other can be just as powerful and will have many of the same benefits.

SECE teacher trainer Sharon Jones has noticed a big difference in how the families of her violin students who have participated in SECE classes before starting lessons understand the benefit of being part of a community.

"In the SECE classes, families learn to support other families. They learn the benefit of encouraging one another and understand the joy of working together cohesively. They discover that by celebrating the small steps of development in other children, they are more able to recognize and celebrate the growth in their own child," she says.

In my own experience, the SECE classes foster an environment of cheering on each other's children and celebrating their accomplishments without any feeling of competition (perhaps because the children are so young), but it carries over into the studio when children start their instruments. It's a good thing to try to emulate in any studio and learn from the SECE classes and a great reason to have a SECE class going in your community.

## Community for Suzuki Parents

It's important to note that it's not just students who benefit from the community that Suzuki lessons provide. As I talked to my colleagues and interviewed teachers for this book, a consistent theme emerged that Suzuki parents benefit as much as the students do.

This method relies a lot on parent involvement in the early stages, probably more than many other activities your child will do. It asks you to understand how your child learns and how to work well with them on a daily basis in practice. In our very independent culture, you as the parent are being asked to be very involved in the learning process and to learn to understand and work well with your child. That is not an easy task. Connecting with other parents working to do the same thing can be so helpful.

Here is what a few experienced Suzuki teachers have found on how community benefits Suzuki parents:

- Alice Joy Lewis emphasized how much the families in her program support each other and each other's children. She has noticed that certain parents in her program really understand the powerful impact of sharing their experience with other parents this way, and do it often. One particular mother in her program has taken on the task of nurturing the other parents and sharing her experiences with them and as a teacher, she can see the powerful impact this has. "It can be so much easier to relate to something another parent tells you about how the process works for them than to just hear it from the teacher," she says.

- Ronda Cole shared that her families build community with one another by getting together to attend concerts, have play dates (outside of group class), and go to other social activities. Group class is the most important community builder for parents and children. Her studio families support each other and even practice with each other's children sometimes. The parents share experiences with one another and really educate each other about what will make them successful in the Suzuki method and in the studio.

- In my studio, I hold a parent talk, or forum, at least once a year to help build community. We always start with parents talking in small groups so they get to know each other beyond whose parent they are. I often hear parents sharing stories with each other of difficult practice times that they have overcome and see how relieved other parents feel to hear it's normal and doesn't have to last forever. I often have parents share things that are working well for them at home with the group. Hearing real life experiences from other parents is reassuring and more relatable than simply hearing it from your teacher.

Don't try to go it alone! Language is best learned by being immersed in an environment of other people speaking it, and music is best learned by being immersed in a community of people making it.

Please, if you aren't already, get involved in your own Suzuki community. If there isn't one where you live, start a small one with other parents around you. Attend events where students play for each other and for the community at large. Make friends with other parents in the studio and share ideas with one another. Get your child together with a buddy from group class to review together or put on a community service concert. There are many ways to join (or create) a community as we learn music together. I encourage you to be a part of it and enjoy the great benefits for your child and yourself.

## Final Thoughts

Teacher trainer Alice Joy Lewis sums it up very well: "The Suzuki community is a significant part of a wholesome approach to music study. It keeps students motivated, and there is so much actual learning that takes place in the group. There is the power of playing together and the power of owning the repertoire. Going out in the community together to perform and play gigs do this too. If parents buy in to the power of community and get their children involved, they are giving themselves and their children a real advantage."

I encourage you to give yourself and your child that advantage. Community involvement as a Suzuki family is not just something that's a good idea if you have the time— it is an integral part of the learning process. Most of us can't stay motivated if we only practice alone for lessons, and our students do not develop an appreciation of the wider music world and how to build ensemble skills if their music education is just one they undertake alone without community. Find a community to get involved in, or start your own little community with a few other families. You will have a huge impact on your child's success by doing so.

That is the power of being an active part of your Suzuki community. It's fun and motivating to be involved in something bigger than ourselves. For many families, having fun and seeing their friends is a good motivator to attend events. Being around others working toward the same goals and who we enjoy being around is a big secret to staying motivated.

I would encourage you to think about being part of a community as part of the to-*be* list rather than the to-do list. Teaching our children to be part of a supportive community is a good life skill and will motivate them to play and keep playing when students go through periods when individual practice feels like a chore. Often, it is the social parts of music (orchestra, group class, etc.) that keep students playing their instrument during times like these.

I saw an example of this recently when the Oregon Suzuki Association got together for our 2015 annual meeting. Almost half of us had grown up as Suzuki students and everyone else had played as children. We broke into small groups and one of the questions we discussed was: What made us love music when we were students?

It was unanimous: each of us had loved music and found the most motivating thing about it was growing up playing with other kids and people. We were all shocked when we realized it wasn't just us, it wasn't just some of us—every single one of us found making music with our peers the most powerful motivator when we were young. It changed the focus of what we wanted to accomplish as an organization and I think it should change our focus as parents.

Find out how you and your child can get involved in the music community around you or find a few like-minded parents and start to build a community where your children get together to play and create your own.

"*Seeing each other regularly at group classes and recitals offers the quiet reinforcement that this journey is worth committing time and energy to, and that we are all in it together.*"

—*Kelly Williamson*

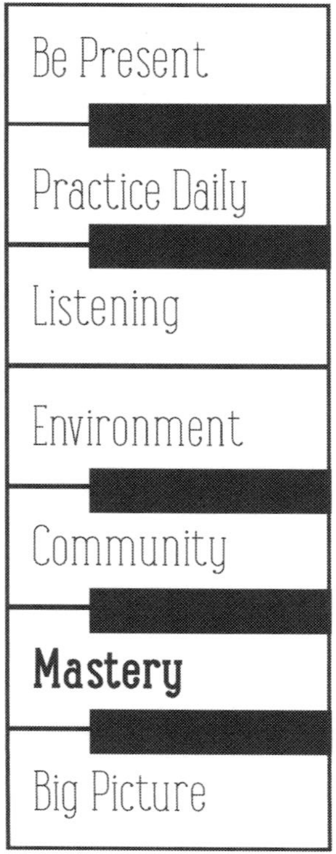
Be Present
Practice Daily
Listening
Environment
Community
Mastery
Big Picture

# Focus on Mastery

9

"Repetition is the single most powerful lever we have to improve our skills ... Embracing repetition means changing your mind-set; instead of viewing it as a chore, view it as your most powerful tool."

—Daniel Coyle, The Little Book of Talent

In more traditional methods of music study, students often focus on learning new material, learning it well, and then moving on to new material. The Suzuki method is different because of its emphasis on review and mastery. In this method, we keep all of our pieces, or at least a large number of them, in our rotation of playable pieces. This way, we can keep coming back to music that is easier to play and use it to work on more advanced skills.

Through this process of review and repetition, we are trying to gain mastery over the skills it takes to play our instrument well. When we're learning a new piece, it may take all our mental energy just to play it correctly. However, when a song is easy to play, we have the ability to concentrate more on technical details like phrasing, style, dynamics, and tone.

I recently had the opportunity to interview virtuoso violinist Rachel Barton Pine and I asked her what she would say to a student who thinks it is time to move on once they've learned the notes and basic technique of a piece.[10] I think her answer gives a great perspective about why to review.

> **Christine Goodner:** Sometimes as teachers, we have students who think, "Well, I've learned the notes and the bowing and the rhythm so now it's time to move on." I would love to hear your thoughts on why it is good to keep coming back to a piece and refining it once you've learned it.

> **Rachel Barton Pine:** If we were athletes and we executed our routine and learned it accurately, then it would be time to move on to the next thing. If we were doing math and figured out that seven plus five equals twelve, then you can't get more perfect than that. In music, the reason we love it so much is that it's an art. Getting everything right is the point at which we actually start working. That's the beginning, not the end.

> Our journey never does end . . . I'm still playing pieces that I learned when I was in the single digits (of age) and finding new things in them: refining my understanding and further clarifying what it is that I want to bring to every moment of emotion.

> And then there is experimentation—that's when it really gets fun! We get to try out different characters, explore our personality in the music,

and just bring it to life. I think it's really great when students do things that they suspect won't work, but they just try it out anyway—not just doing the interpretation that the teacher gives them. It's great to have a teacher who is flexible and will say, "Let's try this—maybe take a little time over here, or maybe take time over here. Which do you like better?"

I think that it's a good idea to find a way to let the performer, even a very young one, have some degree of agency in their repertoire. That way, they are not only "obeying" and doing their best to get it "right," but they are making it specific to themselves. Personalizing their music gets them so excited!

I love her explanation: once we know the basics, then we can start to be artistic and expressive, and truly make music. It's easy, in the process of lessons and daily practice, to feel like just learning a piece is enough and is the ultimate goal. But the main goal is so much more than the basics of getting through the piece. Continuing to work on a piece we already know allows us to really start being artistic and truly making music.

## The Mastery Mindset

Successful families and students are the ones who focus on mastery and developing artistry rather than just getting to the next piece. Progress is not judged by what piece you play, but what skills you have and *how* you play your instrument.

Sometimes it's tempting to compare progress between our own children and others we see around us by asking other parents what piece their child is on or what book they are in. I would argue that doesn't really matter. How well does a student play? Are they playing musically? Are they playing with feeling? That is what is important.

Coming back to the review pieces and playing them as beautifully as possible should be the goal rather than progressing quickly through new music.

## Ownership

Once some basic skills are learned and students can start to play their instrument with ease, students usually start to have more fun playing. At this point, students move beyond working hard to learn a new piece and start to develop a set of music that is very personal to them and that they know inside and out.

With this set of music, students can get together with their peers at institutes, workshops, and play-ins and play together for quite a long time because they have music in common that they all know well. When students gain ownership, the music they are playing becomes *their song,* not just a piece of music they have heard that is unrelated to them. This feeling of ownership is what drives students to practice well on their own as they get older and start to see studying music as something they truly value in their lives.

Here are some of the other main reasons we focus on review and repetition:

- To make hard skills easy.

- To have music in common to play with other people.

- To master the skills needed to play our instrument.

- To build confidence.

- To add advanced technique to music we already know.

- To have pieces ready to play whenever the opportunity to perform arrives.

- To build technique.

## The Science behind Repetition and Making Things Easier

In our culture, we tend to value novelty and consider anything new to be exciting. Especially as adults, many of us love variety and newness. It's important to keep in mind though that children's brains are wired for repetition. Good resources to learn more about the science behind this are Daniel Coyle's books, *The Talent Code* and *The Little Book of Talent*.

In them, he explains in-depth how connections in the brain are strengthened each time a person performs a physical task. The more careful, correct repetitions are practiced, the more easily we can accomplish what we are practicing because the signals being sent from our brain to make the physical task happen can travel so quickly.

Basically practice and review make the connections of our brain stronger and our playing skills more solid. It's hard to argue with that—doing this as a part of each practice is a huge part of building solid skills and that is why Suzuki teachers emphasize it so much. Make sure this is a part of your practice each day. Your teacher will help you come up with a plan, and there are many review charts available online (Google, Pinterest, etc.) to help you get started if you are stuck.

The best thing you can do if you're starting out is to commit to keeping up your review from the beginning. If you do it consistently from the start, your child will have an easy time keeping their pieces easy to play and will have a great foundation on which to build their technique and ability to play musically and artistically. What does this mean? It means all those review pieces that you practice help build the skills within them into quick, easy, efficient skills that can be done with little thinking, allowing musicians to think instead about harder techniques and skills. Technical skills that used to feel challenging become effortless and we forget they were ever hard in the first place because we've done them so much.

## Review (from the Parent Perspective)

While young children crave repetition, as adults we tend to feel the opposite and crave novelty instead. The reality as the practice parent is that all of this emphasis on reviewing material your child had already learned can create a tension between our desire for variety and what we are being asked to do in practice with our children daily. However, we must keep in mind that it is this repetition that helps young players build skills on their instrument and connections in the brain.

When children start playing an instrument at a young age, repeating something many times is often the very thing they crave to do. Young children will gladly play things over and over, especially if we make a game out of it. You may tire of hearing the same thing over and over, but if we don't share those feelings out loud with our children, they will often be perfectly content to do so.

Think about how your child wants to hear the same story over and over again. Or how they ask to watch the same movie time after time. This is the way children's brains work. We, as parents and teachers, should use that to our advantage. By the age when repetition becomes less appealing, we want students to see how much it helps their ability to play and improve. We want them to choose to use it because they can see how much it helps them learn.

As much as you may crave moving on to new things, allow your child to focus on review and repetition. Mastery comes from knowing something and then practicing it until it is automatic. Even before research about the brain could show us why, Suzuki understood this need for repetition. He famously said, "Ability is knowledge plus ten thousand times."

## Ideas for Making Repetitions Easier

So how exactly do we manage to focus on mastery during the day-to-day reality of practice? First, it truly is a shift in our mindset. We need to be willing to let go of feeling pressured to push our children on to the new, exciting piece they are about to learn and focus instead on how we are playing what we already know.

We need to take time over the course of each week to help our children really hone in on what it means to play something with artistry and mastery. I usually recommend that somewhere between one-third to half of my students' practice time is spent on review work. I also emphasize that if you only have a short time to practice and you have to pick one thing on your assignment list to play, I want it to be the review pieces. This is because I know from my experience as a student, and now as a teacher, that the ability to play well comes from this sort of work. There is no shortcut to mastery—it comes from doing something consistently and putting in the practice over time, in order to make it happen.

The following are a few ways to think about how to make review happen in your daily and weekly practice sessions more easily.

## Make Review a Game

Small changes to the way something is repeated can give it some novelty and make it feel new. Playing something three times in each room of the house, or playing something for each stuffed animal around the room are a couple of good examples. A tiny shift in focus like this can make the repetitions feel new again. Remember our goal is to make things easier through practice, and that only comes with enough repetitions that it becomes easy and automatic, rather than simply understanding the concept and moving on.

Counting small items to keep track of repetitions works well for small children. So does rolling the dice to see how many times to repeat something. Students move small items like plastic animals, erasers, or coins from one side of the music stand to another for each repetition. A favorite motivator lately for the three- and four-year-olds I teach is to put a sticker on a blank index card for each repetition.

As students advance and need to complete more repetitions, you can assign a few repetitions to each counter that is moved. There are some great practice games like this in the back of Edmund Sprunger's book *Helping Parents Practice*. I would highly recommend it.

## Have a Review Routine

There are many ways to come up with a routine for your review. Different ideas will appeal to different students and students will also enjoy having a new approach to their routine from time to time to keep things interesting. The most important thing is to realize it needs to be done and follow through to do it.

The following are a few that have worked for my students and for my colleagues' students as well.

- **Review Charts:** There are many charts that can be found online and that rotate the pieces for students to review by the day of the week. This way, the music is divided up for you, and you are sure not to forget anything.

- **Drawing Pieces:** Write the name of each piece to be reviewed on a piece of paper, and the student draws out one piece at a time to see what to review next. You may want to have two containers so the pieces you have most recently played are separate from the ones you haven't played.

- **One Book Per Day:** I recently had a Book Three student who would alternate all his Book One pieces the first day and then all the Book Two pieces the second day back and forth. For him, this was easy to remember and efficient, and it seemed to work really well.

- **Odds & Evens:** My colleague Celeste Okano recently shared this idea: odd number days on the calendar equal odd number pieces in the book to review that day. This is another great way to divide pieces up and get to them all.

# Renewing

Yuko Honda, one of my most influential violin teacher trainers, always emphasized to us that we should focus on *renewing* pieces rather than *reviewing*. How do we play a piece better than we've played before? How do we always improve our skills rather than just repeating mindlessly?

Working to make something better and more beautiful is much more interesting than just running through a list of songs as if it were busywork. Keeping this focus while completing your review portion of practice is a very helpful idea.

It would be incredibly boring, not to mention a waste of time, to play pieces over and over without improving and changing them over time. Every time your child plays a review piece, focus on making it better than the time before. I often recommend working on improving one thing at a time, like tone, and applying that to each review piece on a certain day, or over the course of a week. This way, not only does each song improve, but an aspect of playing our instrument improves overall as well.

Here's one example: my students just completed a bow hold challenge. We worked on our bow holds at the beginning of each lesson and practice and also focused keeping those improved bow holds in place while playing our review pieces. The results were always a better sound. Focusing like this on one thing at a time helps everything a student plays improve. That is using our already-learned pieces to *renew* our playing.

Another way to renew the pieces your child is reviewing is to listen to different versions of the same piece to compare how the song is performed. You will notice that few performers play a piece exactly the same and the awareness that there can be different interpretations of the same piece can really help students, especially advanced students, to see music they are reviewing with renewed interest.

## Giving Students a Motivating Reason to Review

Besides having a focus to review, the most powerful thing you can do to motivate your student to review well is to have a purpose behind it. If there is a compelling reason that the piece should be played and made easier and more beautiful, then students are more invested in doing it. Things like playing group pieces in the next recital with other students or going to institute (Suzuki camp) in the summer and knowing certain review pieces will be expected to be learned well. Here are some other ideas:

- Organize a review concert for family, friends, or a local retirement home. Students can make programs and pick review pieces to perform.

- Hold a review challenge with a fun reward at the end for your own child(ren) or for your students. I have had families find great success with a reward like watching a favorite movie or reading a favorite book with a parent at the end.

- Hold a play-in. Our local Suzuki Association has started having quarterly play-ins. Pieces are chosen, and students from many different teachers come together to play together. For my own students, this is good motivation to be sure the pieces on that list are easy to play and sound as good as possible.

If you see that motivation for review is lagging for you or your child, I would suggest one of these ideas. Also, ask your own teacher for ideas they may have. Have a reason to get those pieces sounding the best your child can possibly make them, and then motivation for practicing them can really take off.

## Final Thoughts

Making time to keep review pieces easy while consistently improving them is one of the habits of successful Suzuki families. Keep a mindset of mastery, not a mindset of learning new things quickly, and then leaving them behind. Through revisiting pieces and renewing them on a consistent basis, your child's ability to play their instrument with ease will grow. What your child can play is not nearly as important as *how* your child can play. As teachers and parents alike, it is important to stay focused on that—especially when it is our tendency to have the most fun with new and novel things as adults.

Build a good review habit from the start and help your child stay motivated to review by giving them opportunities to participate in events where they are asked to perform these pieces at a high level of playing skill. This will go a long way toward their success as Suzuki students.

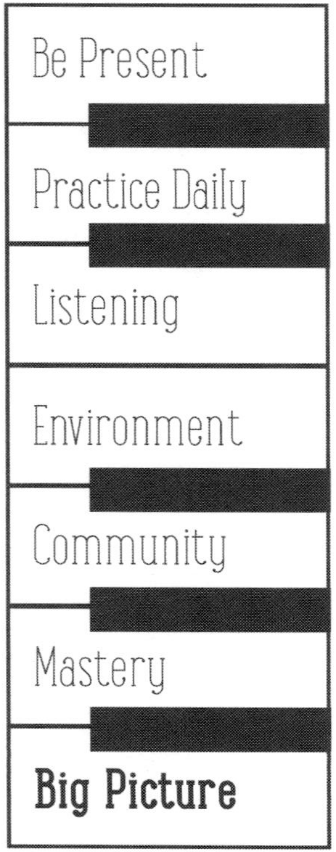
Be Present
Practice Daily
Listening
Environment
Community
Mastery
Big Picture

# Focus on the Big Picture

**10**

It's easy to get lost in all the details and miss the big picture when there are so many different things to keep in mind as your child is learning their instrument. It can seem like a long journey to go from where your child is now to the more advanced stages of playing that you see in older students.

Over-focusing on the small details now can cause us to lose perspective on the bigger picture of what we are doing over many years, both musically and in our children's overall character development.

Each week, your teacher will send you home with practice assignments, often with one overarching theme for the week (or per assignment). These themes tell you what your teacher thinks should be your big-picture focus right now. Sometimes it's tempting to ignore these instructions from the teacher and focus on things that we as parents feel are more important at the moment. Please remember that a good teacher will have a long-term vision in mind for how to get your child from where they are now to more advanced stages of playing their instrument. Ignoring these big-picture ideas (that your teacher is trained in and experienced in) will slow down progress and stunt growth in the long run, even if they seem to be getting in the way of going faster now. Remember that your teacher is trying to help your child develop as a musician and there are many steps along the way through that process.

Professor Robert Duke (University of Texas, Austin) sums this up well in his book, *Intelligent Music Teaching.*[11] He says, "Learning to play or sing any scale, any exercise, or any piece is never the real goal of music instruction, even though teachers sometimes verbalize this as their goals. The real goal—the meaningful, substantive, far-reaching goal— is for students to become superb musicians, doing all of the things that superb musicians do, irrespective of what is being played or sung at the moment."

This is a great way to look at the big picture both musically and developmentally. Whatever small thing we are working on, we are *really* working on being great musicians and (I would add) great human beings as well.

Beyond what your teacher emphasizes in lessons each week, there are three big-picture items that Suzuki parents should always keep in mind: tone, technique-building, and character development.

## Big-Picture Focus: Tone

There are many things to focus on while practicing. Suzuki himself emphasized focusing attention on one thing at a time while practicing. If you are in doubt of what that one thing is, work on tone.

Tone is defined (by the *Merriam-Webster Dictionary*) as "the quality of sound produced by a musical instrument or singing voice." Tone goes beyond playing in tune. How warm is the sound? Does it have a ringing quality or harsh quality to it? Is it communicating something through music?

Beautiful tone is hard to describe, but we tend to know it when we hear it. It is the kind of sound that makes music pleasing to the ear and helps communicate emotion and feeling. Very simply, you can think of this concept as playing with a beautiful sound.

Review pieces, especially the easy ones, are another great place to focus on tone. How does each note of a piece sound? Are certain notes (or notes on certain strings for string players) more beautiful-sounding than others? How can we make every note beautiful? This is a long-term project that is worth working on. Anyone can rush through the notes and get to the end. A good musician tells a story, shares a feeling, and makes a beautiful sound with the instrument.

Depending on your instrument, the techniques, and the exercises you will need to master to have beautiful tone will vary. But focusing on this as part of the big picture will be important for whatever you play.

Many teachers help students develop tone by using Suzuki's tonalization exercise, having students play on open strings (for string players) or warming up with scales. Sometimes we can be anxious to move on to other parts of practice and to shortchange these less exciting assignments; however, it is here that students develop the ability to play with a beautiful sound. It's not just busywork to complete these warm-up assignments; it is often where we can develop tone best.

## Big-Picture Focus: Technique-Building

Another part of the big picture is a focus on technique. Each time you learn a new piece as a Suzuki student, you are learning the technique to play your instrument well.

That may seem like a very obvious statement, but it is easy to get so focused on learning new pieces and music that we forget to use those songs to build up our ability to play well.

Suzuki teacher trainer (and a pioneer of the Suzuki method in America) John Kendall famously has his teacher trainees pound the table and repeat, "We use the pieces to teach the technique! We use the pieces to teach the technique!" As teachers, we have to keep this in mind every time we teach, and as parents, we also need to keep it in mind every time we practice. It is easy to lose focus on the fact that technique-building is one of our primary goals.

Pay close attention to posture, hand positions, and the other little details of playing that your teacher talks about in lessons each week. This is what will support your ability to play more advanced music later!

Rushing through and just learning the notes in the correct order without attention to how the instrument is being played will create big problems later. There is so much more to becoming a musician than learning notes. Trust your teacher: when they are slowing you down to talk about little details, it is often with the bigger picture of developing technique in mind.

It may be hard to see why little technical details are important now, but all of the skills you are building now will help you develop the technique level to succeed later.

Teacher trainer Kelly Williamson shared that during her early years as a teacher, she developed what she called the "Golden Question." She asked herself, "What does this child need from me right now?" As a fellow parent, I encourage you to ask yourself this question often.

## Big-Picture Focus: Character Development

It's important to step back and look at the character traits we are developing while studying music as part of the big picture as well. There can be many ups and downs while a student learns an instrument. Times when motivation is high and accomplishments are easy to see, and also times when nothing seems to be happening and frustration levels are high. Your child is developing who they are as a person through all of these different outcomes and emotions. Sometimes when we don't see much progress musically; it is wise to stand back and look at what else our child is learning.

- You may wish your child was in a different level group class or orchestra, but sometimes being the most advanced in a group is what allows a student to develop confidence and leadership skills.

- Your child may not feel like practicing today, even though there is plenty of time to do so. But following through and doing at least some kind of practice teaches them commitment to their goals and discipline.

- Your child may be on the same piece for a long time and it may seem like they just can't wrap their head around how to master the skills the teacher is asking them to in order to move on. But by coming back to the challenge again and again, your child may learn to keep approaching problems with different possible solutions until something works.

I could go on and on with examples, and you may be able to think of a few examples that specifically apply to your situation. Sometimes, when problems come up, there isn't a clear answer for what to do, but there may be a clear answer for developing good character in our children or students. It's an important part of the big picture to keep in mind.

We may feel tempted to give up and stop playing when musical progress isn't happening as quickly or as easily as we want. But this is shortsighted; often the roadblocks you will come up against in practicing your instrument are the same ones your child will also encounter with some difficult subject at school or in some other area of life.

Successful Suzuki families know that success is made up of lots of tiny, sometimes-hard-to-see victories all added up together. It's learning to be calm and focused. It's learning to hold the instrument (and all the little steps involved). It's learning to recognize the sound different notes make and how to produce that sound on a consistent basis. I could go on and on.

It's not so important that every day is perfect or that every piece of the puzzle is perfect. What we are trying to develop are great human beings who also play great music. *That* is the big picture.

Who will my child be in ten or twenty years because we've been on this journey? Who has being a musician, to the best of my child's ability, caused them to become as people in the world?

Suzuki's vision was to develop great people with beautiful hearts. How are we as teachers and parents causing that to be developed in our children and students?

## The Big Picture: What Your Child Needs

What does your child need from you to help them focus on the big picture? It may be help staying focused on what your teacher wants you to improve through practice this week. It may be a technical problem you are trying to solve. But it also very well may be encouragement, and unwavering belief that they are capable, or simply to know that you are there and enjoy the time you are spending with them.

"Sometimes we have to be able to see beyond challenging practices when they happen and see what we're doing as part of the bigger pictures" says Williamson. The Suzuki philosophy explains it very clearly, when Dr. Suzuki says that progress takes place at each student's own pace. Where we are right now is exactly where we are supposed to be."

## Checking In on the Big Picture with Your Teacher

One way I like to help families in my studio get refocused on the big picture is by holding parent-teacher conferences once a year. It's a time to step back and look at what has been accomplished, where we're headed, and what course corrections we may want to make to get the results we're looking for.

This is really individual because different students learn at different rates, face different challenges to overcome, and have different goals. I have found that talking one-on-one and getting on the same page with one another helps us all understand each other's perspectives and goals and what we can do to help the student succeed.

Even if your teacher doesn't hold these types of conferences for their whole studio, most teachers would be open to a request for your family or child. It would certainly be worth asking about.

I also recommend attending any Suzuki parent talks offered in your area, by your teacher, or in the larger community. I try to offer at least one parent talk during each school year for my studio families, and it is the families that come to these types of events that I feel really understand how to help their children best.

In my talks, I often pick a topic that I think is most needed by parents in my studio or that I have recently learned more about and want to share. It's a great way to focus the whole studio on the big picture in some form. Not all teachers offer this—it is a new addition to my studio over the last couple of years.

If your teacher doesn't offer them, I would look to your bigger Suzuki community for resources like this. The Suzuki Association of the Americas (SAA) puts on a yearly online video series for parents called "Parents as Partners" where short talks are shared on how to help make the Suzuki journey work a little better for your family. I would highly recommend it.

Also, reading books like this one or Suzuki blogs are great ways to keep thinking beyond your own lessons and practice sessions each week. It's good to get a new perspective from time to time and to refocus on what is most important when we are practicing with our children.

## Make a Progress List

I would encourage all parents to make a list of the things your child has learned since starting their instrument (or in the last year, even). You can include actual instrumental skills, music theory, or reading skills and for sure character development that you've seen happen.

If you're like most families, you will come up with quite an extensive list. This is great to keep in mind when it feels like practice is a daily slog or it's hard to step out of the day-to-day details and see the big picture of what music is doing for your child. Often, it's very encouraging to see how much progress has been made. The reality is that it's very hard to see it happening when we look from day to day. It's very much like seeing a picture of our children from a year or two ago—we haven't noticed a huge change because we've seen them every day but looking back we think, "Wow! Look how young they were!" and are amazed at the changes.

## Final Thoughts

So what are we trying to focus on when we talk about the big picture? It really is a mix between musical and personal skills. We are on a long-term journey to improve upon both.

It's important not to get too worried about where we are right now, but rather to notice how far we have come and have faith that we will continue to grow. What are we developing in our children as musicians and as people through our lessons, daily practice, and other habits as musicians?

You can find a list of character qualities I have seen students develop at http://www.suzukitriangle.com/50-character-qualities-developed-in-music-students/. How have you seen your child grow in these areas?

Some Suzuki students will go on to be professional musicians, but many will go on to a variety of other careers. What ever our children end up doing in life can be positively impacted by their studies in music. Being people of character, learning to work hard, learning to be sensitive, and giving attention to detail—these are all parts of being a wonderful human being, which, after all, really is the goal of the Suzuki method.

So focus on this: How far has your child or student come on their instrument? How have you seen them develop as people? How can you help them make big strides in both of these areas as their teacher or parent? As Kelly Williamson so nicely put it, *We are exactly where we are supposed to be.*

# Final Thoughts

11

This book has been a study of the different ways you can adopt the habits and mindset of families who succeed in the Suzuki method. I am passionate about helping get this information to parents and teachers and have spent years trying to find the best ways to share this information with them. This book came about as a way to do that.

This is intended to be a practical, parent-friendly guide to help make the Suzuki method work in your daily life as a Suzuki family. It is the kind of guide I wish I had had when I was a Suzuki parent myself.

While this book is meant to be a basic look at the different habits and the mindset that helps families succeed, it certainly doesn't cover every possible topic or every family's circumstances. I am certain that more can be said about each of the topics discussed here, and I encourage parents and teachers to use this book as a starting point to begin conversations that are more specific to your individual situation. I hope everyone is able to add your own stories and wisdom to the conversation.

There are a few final thoughts I would like to end with.

Growing up as a Suzuki student is an important part of my identity. The lessons I learned about myself and life from practicing daily with my parents, working with great teachers, making music with my peers, and learning to work through hard things shaped who I am—far beyond my ability to play the violin and viola.

I was very fortunate to have parents who understood the concepts in this book. *Who* I was growing up to be was much more important to them than any short-term goals they had for me, and certainly more important than how I performed on my instrument or how fast I learned new music. I was, however, expected to always do my best. I think the balance between those two things is vitally important.

All of the Suzuki teacher trainers I interviewed emphasized that success in this method means developing each student as a person, not just developing their musical skills. What greater calling do we have as parents than to do the same?

The aspects of the Suzuki method that help students succeed like practicing daily, being present, listening to great music, being an active part of the community, creating a positive and nurturing environment, and focusing on the big picture will help you do exactly that.

My wish for Suzuki families is that they will use what their children are learning in this method to help them reach their potential on their instrument and as a human being.

I hope reading this book helps you do just that.

# RESOURCES

**More on the Suzuki Method:**

www.SuzukiAssociation.org

**Favorite Suzuki Blogs:**

www.PluckyViolinTeacher.com
www.TeachSuzuki.blogspot.com
www.SuzukiExperience.com
www.ChiliDogStrings.com

**Suzuki Early Childhood Education:**

https://suzukiassociation.org/ece/
http://suzukiece.com/Pages/links.htm

# ACKNOWLEDGMENTS

This is a project I could not have done without a huge support system. If you listened to me talk about it, cheered me on, or offered ideas in any way, you have my heartfelt thanks! I also want to specifically thank the following people:

First I would like to thank my amazing editor Shayla Eaton for your time and expert help getting this book ready to publish.

Thank you to designer Melinda Martin for her help making this book look amazing, including the cover and formatting.

Thank you to the teacher trainers who generously gave their time and expertise to this project: Ronda Cole, Sharon Jones, Alice Joy Lewis, Ann Montzka-Smelser, and Kelly Williamson.

Thank you to my dad and brothers (Thomas D Wilson, Richard C. Wilson, and Charles B Wilson) who shared their publishing and book writing knowledge with me and helped with feedback all along the way.

A huge thank-you to my husband Mike for his unending support—you never think my wild ideas are too crazy to try.

Wendy Knight: for being a lifelong friend, first reader, and talking through the process with me during all the ups and downs of this process.

Thank you to the Suzuki parents and teachers who added their input, including: Alan Duncan, Lauren Lamont, Lisa Hansen, Michele Monahan Horner, Jody Morrissette, Celeste Okano, Jo-Anne Steggall, and Namrata Sharma.

Thank you to a crew of friends who listened and made suggestions on an ongoing basis: Liz Peyton, Angel Falu Garcia, Jen Gillette, Rebekah Hanson, and Danette Schuh.

Thank you to all the amazing teachers in the Oregon Suzuki Association for sharing your ideas and making our community an awesome one.

And for all of my own Suzuki teachers and teacher trainers: thank you for teaching me to play, to teach and to help share the spirit of Dr. Suzuki.

# ABOUT THE AUTHOR

Christine Goodner is a dynamic and experienced Suzuki teacher with over 18 years of experience in music education. Her unique blend of expertise in music, child development, and leadership gives her a holistic approach to working with teachers, students, and their parents. Christine holds a degree in Early Childhood Education, and has extensive teacher training through the Suzuki Association of the Americas (SAA). She teaches violin, viola, and Suzuki ECE in Hillsboro, Oregon, and is currently serving as President of the Oregon Suzuki Association.

You can read more of her writing and find updates on new projects on her blog www.SuzukiTriangle.com.

# SOURCES

## (Endnotes)

1   Daniel Coyle, *The Talent Code: Greatness Isn't Born. It's Grown. Here's How* (Bantam Books: New York, New York, 2009).

2   Ibid, pg. 104.

3   Alan Duncan, SuzukiExperience.com.

4   Shin'ichi Suzuki, *Nurtured by Love* (Alfred Music Publishing Company: Van Nuys, California, 2012).

5   Angela Duckworth, *Grit: The Power of Passion and Perseverance* (Scribner: New York, New York, 2016).

6   Judith Stein, Lynn Meltzer, Kalyani Krishnan, Laura Pollica, *Parent Guide to Hassle-Free Homework: Proven Practices that Work—from Experts in the Field*

7   Gretchen Rubin, *Better Than Before: What I Learned About Making and Breaking Habits—to Sleep More, Quit Sugar, Procrastinate Less, and Generally Build a Happier Life* (Broadway Books: New York, New York, 2015).

8   Michele Monahan Horner, *Life Lens: Seeing Your Children in Color* (MCP Books: Minneapolis, Minnesota, 2016).

9   Ibid.

10  Christine Goodner, "Artistry, Inspiration, and Suzuki Parenting: An Interview with Rachel Barton Pine," Suzuki Association of the Americas. Published November 1, 2016. Accessed March 29, 2017. https://suzukiassociation.org/news/artistry-inspiration-suzuki-parenting-interview/.

11  Robert Duke, *Intelligent Music Teaching: Essays on the Core Principles of Effective Instruction* (Learning and Behavior Resources: Austin, Texas, 2007).

Made in the
USA
Monee, IL